# Praise for The Big Dog Diaries

*"I read this book quite by accident. A friend gave it to me and while I was eating lunch one day, I casually read the first few pages and was hooked by this big ugly dog's story. Anyone who is a dog lover will fall in love with Big."* - Andrew C. Palmer

*"A very quick (too quick!) read. I love Laz's style. If you are looking for one of those annoyingly cloying books about a cutesy dog, try something else. If you want gritty realism, try something else. If you want a delightfully droll read, then settle in for a very pleasant time. I'm going to make this my go-to book when gifting people who like animals."* - Mary L. Herrick

*"I had a hard time putting [the book] down. Written in a unique style, this is a book that dog people, runners, walkers, and everybody else with a heart will enjoy."* - Harald Vaessin "HEFV"

*"A story about a pit bull dog may be offputting to some; but one must forget all the negative things associated with this breed in this case. Lazarus Lake is a great storyteller. His prose style is different from probably anything you have read before; but it flows smoothly and keeps the reader interested. Whether big is as special as he seems because of his genetics, or the training he received from laz, or a combination of the two is not important to the quality of the stories. He provides entertainment for his human family; and these stories shall provide great entertainment for all those fortunate enough to read them."* - Dan Baglione

# the big dog diaries

*part 1: my name is big*
*part 2: big adventures*
*part 3: big tails*

# the big dog diaries
# part 2: big adventures

## Lazarus Lake

Illustrations by Betsy Julian

laz.btsgifts.com
drystoneman@hotmail.com

First Printed Edition, October 2012

Printed in the United States of America
Print ISBN-10: 1480028169
Print ISBN-13: 978-1480028166
BISAC: Pets / Dogs / Breeds

Illustrations by Betsy Julian

Published by Trail Trotter Press / Run to Win, LLC (the "Publisher").

Trail Trotter Press
824 Roosevelt Trail #203
Windham, ME, 04062
www.TrailTrotterPress.com

# Table of Contents

## Prologue:

*hello, my name is big.*
*i have a very good life.*
*i have a kind master, who takes very good care of me.*
*i have important work to do.*

*i live with my family*
*at their house in the woods.*
*i have my own place to sleep,*
*and plenty to eat.*
*i always have fresh water.*
*sometimes i get treats.*

*and best of all,*
*many people love me,*
*and i get lots of petting.*

*i am a very happy dog.*

*my life was not always this good.*
*sometimes my first master was mean to me.*
*one day he took me for a ride*
*and forgot me here in the woods.*

*i got shot.*

*i was hungry*
*and thirsty*
*and hurt...*

*and very alone.*

*then the kind master found me.*
*i knew this would be my home*
*and i would belong to the kind master.*

*but many other things happened first.*
*the kind master taught me how to be a good dog.*
*i was very happy.*

but one day a man came and took me away from my kind master.
i left to live with a young master, far from home.
for a long time i stayed with the young master.
then one day he took me for a long ride
and forgot me.

then i had no master.
i was chained in a yard, all alone.
children threw rocks at me.
sometimes no one remembered to feed me.
and worst of all, no one petted me.

but one day my family found me.
and i came back to live with the kind master.
this time i was home to stay.
i was the happiest dog i could be.

since then my master and i have had many adventures.
after we have adventures he writes them down,
to share with my many friends.

these are my stories.
i hope you enjoy them.

Big

## october 30, 2011
## it's for the kids

big & i did a new 5-miler today.
we walked to millersburg & back.

its a good route.
other than the trailer dogs, we only encountered one other dog,
and it wasn't a problem dog.

there was an older gentleman out working on his car just before
we got to millersburg,
and he had one of those maltese dogs outside with him.
(looks kind of like a pug, but with short legs and long hair)

the man's head was under the hood, so he didn't see us,
but his dog did, and it came "running" out to the road.
the man pulled his head out from under the hood and looked
around only to see his dog & big standing in the road sniffing
noses.

he came out to the road with great haste,
calling his dog.
i tried to ease his concern;
"it's ok, he likes other dogs."

no answer.

by then the man was close enough that his dog responded and
went to him,
big turned, wagging his tail at the man.
i added;
"he likes people, too."

no answer.

the man scooped up the malty & hurried away, stealing glances
at us over his shoulder.

"sorry big, not everyone wants to pet you."

3

big just looked at me and wagged his tail.
it isn't the first time he's gotten that treatment.

we'll be walking that way again.
it is a nice route.
every time we see the man,
we'll wave at him.
(and big will wag his tail)

eventually he will wave back.
i doubt he'll ever come out & pet big.

here it is Halloween, and no one has knocked at our door tonight.
if you really don't want trick or treaters,
let it be known that a big resides at your house.
(the half-mile hike between houses out here probably doesn't
help our chances)
on the other hand,
we aren't likely to get our yard rolled, either.

laz

## november 1, 2011
## big and the rainbow raiders

the other day i went out for an interview.
not a real interview, but one of those sales jobs
where they hope to extract money from you.

i knew it was a pointless trip,
but back when i was hitchhiking around the country i had
learned about invisibility.
if you stand in one place hitchhiking for too long,
you fade into the scenery.
people can no longer see you and you'll never get a ride.
so if you stand in one place for a couple of hours you need to
walk down the road a ways,
that way people can see you again.

i figured job-hunting is a lot the same way.
and i needed to do something (anything) so i wouldn't become
invisible.
it had started coming down a cold rain when i pulled up in the
drive.
big was snug in his bigloo, but sophie & little were in the pen.

there is a cover over one corner of the pen,
which provides some shelter from the rain,
but little & sophie have different approaches to rain in the pen.
little huddles under the cover, where it is dry.
sophie stands next to the gate,
and barks for someone to come get her.

so when i drive up, there they are.
sophie, soaking wet, is standing at the gate barking at the empty
house.
little is curled up in the corner, watching me.

little isn't going to move until i open the gate *and* call her.
sophie isn't going to get out of the rain until someone lets her out
of the pen.

5

i figured they would just head for the porch as soon as i let them
out. that's what they usually do when it is raining.
so i went to rescue them,
still in my good clothes...

error!

apparently, while i was gone and before the rain began,
they had been watching big chew on his bones.
he has a half a rhinocerus femur
(seeing him bite a 2-inch bone in half reminded me why i keep
him in controlled situations)
and a hippopitamus hip joint that his pal shannon brought him
during the backyard ultra.
unknown to me, sophie & little had cooked up a plot.

as soon as i gave the word to come out,
they shot out of the pen,
and instead of racing to the porch
they made a beeline for big's place.

big saw what was happening, and came tearing out of his bigloo
to defend his possessions but little was on the hippo hip in a
flash.

however, it was too large for her to snatch up on the run.
she grabbed it once, and it slipped out of her mouth.
she had time for one more attempt before big was on top of her,
she darted away at the last second, the bone slipping from her
grip again.

as big turned to chase little,
sophie darted in to take a stab at the rhinocerus femur.
just like little, she found the bone too large to grab.
big wheeled around and came after sophie.

just like she has for dealing with the rain, sophie has different
tactics for dealing with big.
as soon as she saw him coming for her,
she dropped to the ground, and rolled onto her back.

6

big rushed over & began trying to push her to her feet with his
nose so they could play "the game."

by this time, i had reached the big perimeter
and was standing there swearing at the dogs for dragging me out
into the rain & mud in my good clothes;
"next time you'll stay in the rain until i change, you idiots!"

as fast as big could roll sophie over,
she flipped back onto her back,
and there we stood in a freezing rain.
big pushing sophie in circles on her back in the mud,
and me standing at the edge of the mud, swearing.

little took the distraction as an opportunity to rush in behind big,
like a jackal
and while watching big intently, little rolled the hippo hip around
until she got a grip on a piece of tendon.
then she raced away, proudly carrying her prize.

big saw little fleeing, and abandoned his futile attempts to get
sophie to her feet, chasing (with equal futility) after little.
sophie jumped up, but instead of running away,
she went back for the prized rhino femur.
when big saw that he came rushing back...
and the whole get sophie off her back routine started anew.

i had to tiptoe out, trying to step on rocks (fortunately abundant
up on the hill) and drag sophie out by her collar,
holding her at arms length;
while simultaneously warning big not to jump up on me.

i finally got the two miscreants up on the porch,
dried little off and washed all the mud off sophie
and sent them in the house before returning big his hippo hip
(at which point he happily returned to his repose in the bigloo).

miraculously there was not a speck of mud on my good clothes.
i am pretty certain that all 3 dogs were laughing.

laz

## november 04, 2011
## the big test

> Maybe Big should move inside the house with you guys.
> Just sayin;
>     Larry

you havent seen big play.
a tornado would make an equally suitable house pet.

the big guy was resting on his laurels today.
having been on his best behavior recently, he must have decided
it was time to use up some of his credits.

when amy took him out to run he took off after one of the short
hares and pulled her into the ditch.
that earned him a quick return home.

when i took him out for his 5 mile walk,
we spent the most of the walk with me saying;
"big, quit pulling. BIG, CUT IT OUT!"

when we got home he still had excess energy.
now that it has turned cool, big has a lot more spunk.
so we had a play session.

i leaned over & slapped my knees with both hands;
"go go go go go big, go go go go go"
his face lit up with joy and he tucked his butt and tore around his
area at 90 miles an hour.
i was jumping over the whipping cable like a frog on a hot plate.

"go go go go go"

he would come running straight at me,
then leap 4 feet in the air as he went past
(he can't jump on me, but he loves to jump past me)
he made 90 degree turns, sending rocks & dirt flying.
he ran headfirst into his bigloo at top speed
the bigloo bouncing around as he somehow

9

(with loud thumps & bumps)
made a 180 & emerged still at top speed.
around and around he went,
every time he slowed down i would yell;
"go go go go go!"
and he would tear off with renewed vigor.

after about 10 minutes of this
big trotted over, sat next to me, & leaned against my legs panting.
after a little petting he had caught his breath enough to head to
the bigloo for a nap.

big a house dog??

you haven't seen him play.

laz

**november 09, 2011**
**the bigwich**

for all the dozens of times the big has removed his "dogproof"
collar, he has yet to remove it when we aren't home.

at first that seems surprising,
but it really is exactly what you would expect.
he knows he is supposed to wear it,
he only takes it off when we mess up the schedule.
the schedule must be honored.

there was a death in the family,
and the schedule was disrupted.
sunday we had to go to visitation in clarksville...
an event that took all afternoon & most of the night.
we got up early and squeezed in big's walking & running.
i had mine all planned out, and walked little while amy ran
then i took big on a good 5 mile walk.
there was even a special event for big.

the goat corner dog has been gradually working up its courage.
after i administered a lesson with my dog trainer last year,
it wanted no part of me & my dogs.
after a few months it gathered up enough nerve to bark at us
from inside the backyard fence.
eventually it moved to the garage,
then finally out into the yard beside the road.

big has done an admirable job ignoring it,
except for (of course) leaving a pee-mail after we pass
and kicking dirt in its direction.

this maddens the goat corner dog.
it is a good sized dog,  and is accustomed to kicking the other
dogs' butts in its neighborhood.

the last time we passed, it got so mad when big did that,
it came out in the road behind us and barked.
big looked at him, then pooped and kicked dirt.

11

goat corner dog was beside himself...
sometimes big's messages aren't so discreet.

anyway, sunday the goat corner dog was all the way in the ditch.
i was impressed as big scarcely glanced in that direction,
because goat corner was getting pretty close.
he stopped at the end of his yard,
and we walked about 50 yards further before stopping for big to
send a pee mail.

something snapped in the goat corner dog.
baying furiously, he came tearing down the road after us.
big might only have 4 toes, but he was definitely giving goat
corner the finger (again),
and goat corner wasn't going to take it any more.

i had a surprise for both dogs.
little has been the only one with me when i have had to get more
aggressive.
little was the one with me when i gave goat corner lesson 1 with
my dog trainer.
big has never been along when contemptuous ignoring was
insufficient.
maybe a discreet raising of the tip of the dog trainer.

when goat corner got within about 20 feet i wheeled and
charged, dog trainer raised to full striking position;
"you want to chase us down the road, you son of a lizard?"

goat corner dog suddenly remembered the fading lesson.
he turned around so fast his front end was headed back up the
road for the yard before his tail end finished coming towards us.

"i'll knock your teeth down your throat, you fool."
goat corner dog fled in terror, all the way to his yard.
i pursued about 30 feet and stopped to watch until he was all the
way back home.

big is very good at moving exactly with me (when he wants to
be) and he had gone thru the whole thing with such excellent
choreography

that it was like i had no dog on the leash.
i looked down at big,
and he was looking back at me with this amazed expression.
like i was even more powerful than he had imagined.
the rest of the walk was excellent.

yesterday was a different story.
we had to go back for the funeral,
and we were going to leave early, and be gone all day.
i got up extra early again to take both dogs for short walks.

amy needed a day off, so there was no run.
little had stolen big's rhino leg bone and hidden it in the woods
on saturday, so i found it and set it aside on the back porch.
when we were ready to leave, i gave it to amy to return to the
big, sort of a consolation prize for missing his run.

he was tickled pink to get his precious bone back,
but when amy started to leave with no run happening,
he was heartbroken.
as she walked away, he started to cry.
you haven't heard sad till you've heard big cry.
it isn't very loud, but it is a heartrending keening that is hard to
get out of your mind.

this morning i knew what to expect.
if big gets "forgotten" one day,
he is not about to let it happen two days in a row.
when amy left to run with sophie,
i went on out to the back porch and waited.

for a few minutes big barked furiously;
"why, why are you running with that inferior dog?"
then it got ominously quiet.
sure enough, i soon heard the thundering sound of a big coming
around the house at full speed.

he had his head up, looking anxiously down the driveway,
but when i hollered at him,
he quickly turned to come up on the porch.
we sat a while and talked.

13

i sat on the step and he sat between my feet,
then he leaned his head back against me,
so i could rub his throat & scratch his chest.
after a while he rolled completely on his back,
so i could rub his belly.

finally he got to wallering around too much so i made him move.
then he sat beside me, put one front leg over my leg,
and rested his massive head on my knee.
he was one content big.

when amy got home, she went and got his collar,
and we all sat on the porch a little while.
amy on one side, me on the other
big in the middle, like the meat in a sandwich.
he loves the bigwich position.

he got his long run with amy,
then i took him for a lap of the big trail.
at the end he was pleasantly exhausted.
after a good breakfast he was ready for a leisurely afternoon of
laying in the sun...

attached to his cable.
that means we are in charge....

right?

laz

## november 14, 2011
## big don't care

honey badger move over.
big don't care either.

amy & i were both disappointed when the rain was late this
morning
(it still hasn't arrived)
big needs a day off.
his steady diet of 7-10 mile days has aggravated his bad shoulder
and every day he limps a little worse.
but big don't care.

he wants to run every day
and he wants to run far.
no matter how beat he is, he is ready for more.
i can come home in 98 degree heat,
big trailing behind,
puffing like a steam engine,
struggling to keep up,
and when we reach the driveway he wants to go straight,
and start another one of our courses.

when we walk by the trailhead,
he tries get me to turn onto the trail.
if we'd allow it, big would walk till he dropped dead.
so a little thing like a painful shoulder is not going to discourage
him at all.

he will (reluctantly) accept not getting to keep a walk going
forever, but big does not easily accept days off.
if it rains, he knows we aren't going
and everything is ok.
but if it ain't raining....

he takes off his "escape proof" collar and comes looking for us.

so, a crippled shoulder?
big don't care.

15

some things he does care about.
he doesn't like amy taking sophie out to run first.
i think the first part is what agitates him.
he doesn't fuss when i take little walking....
*after* big has already been.

big is supposed to go first,
because big is the number one dog.
he isn't always trying to prove who is the number one dog,
like little and sophie are.
he just takes it as a given.

he isn't jealous if we pet little or sophie,
the other one is on the spot trying to push in between.
call sophie, she might come or she might not.
if you want sophie to come for sure, you call for little.
sophie always comes when someone calls for little.

little can be pretty aloof.
neither the jack russell part, nor the bull terrier part of her came
with an inclination to be cuddly all the time.
but if you pet another dog, little suddenly needs to be held.
when i am out taking care of big,
i can see little sitting in the window...
watching intently.
or sophie and little together in the pen...
watching intently.

big is indifferent if you pet another dog...
big don't care.

when he is on a mission, big don't care about pain.
he would walk till his leg fell off.
he would defend his humans to the death without hesitation.
when he thought mr winston's dog was about to bite amy,
he was on a mission.
it was as if i were not attached to his leash, giving commands
i even smacked him a good one with my dog trainer,
trying to get his attention.
if he so much as felt it, i couldn't tell.
that is something to remember about pit bulls.

16

one shot with my dog trainer has been reliable in terminating
dog aggression.
it has been known to leave much larger dogs than big with
permanent emotional scars.

it did not even make big blink.
good thing my authority over big is not based on force or fear.

on the other hand,
when he isn't on a mission,
big does care about men with sticks.
ben has a stick he carries when he runs
(sort of a dog trainer without the "pop")

big knows this.
when ben and i cross paths on our morning run,
we always stop and talk.
big watches ben's stick like a hawk,
and subtly moves about to keep me between him and it.

ben saw big watching the stick the other morning,
so he hid it behind his back.
i told ben;
"that won't work with big. he still knows you have a stick."

big is not a sophie.
you can take sophie's binky out of her mouth,
hide it behind your back,
and ask; "where is your binky, sophe?"
she goes over and looks up at the fireplace mantle.
after all, that is where we put toys when little and sophie
misbehave with them.

not that we will be playing the binky trick on sophie any more.
little swallowed the binky.
it wasn't easy.

a tennis ball cover doesn't lend itself to going down but little
thinks anything that will fit in your mouth might be food.
unfortunately, we caught on too late.
one moment little had stolen sophie's binky

and was parading about with it.
the next minute she was struggling to get something swallowed
and the binky was gone.

"little, you idiot!"
"don't you ever learn?"
"the harder something is to swallow, the harder it is to pass."
and we have seen little both swallow and pass some pretty
remarkable things.

if i laugh at the sight (and it can be pretty funny)...

little don't care.

laz

## november 16, 2011
## coach big takes me running

the rain we'd been hoping for so big would rest his bad shoulder
took its sweet time getting here.

it still hadn't arrived this morning
(almost 36 hours after it had been predicted)
amy didn't take big running this morning...

he might not accept a day off,
but amy was past ready for one.
i looked at the radar
and saw that the rain was almost to us,
but i decided to take big walking
(at least until the rain started)

he was outside barking his alarm that it was time we got to work
and i was going to be gone most of the day.
we were spending the afternoon with aunt mae at the nursing
home (they were having their thanksgiving dinner)
and after that we were going to a basketball game on the other
side of nashville.

i couldn't stand to leave poor big alone all day.
 he was (as always) overjoyed to see me coming with his blue
leash.

*woooh, woooh, woooh*
he greeted me
a joyous grin splitting his huge head in two.
then he was leaping head high with excitement
before finally forcing himself to sit, quivering,
while i hooked him up.
as we passed the porch,
i picked up my umbrella and warned him;
"if it starts to rain, we'll have to come home."

usually running with amy takes some of big's energy off the top

so he was struggling to keep from pulling when we started out
with him fresh.

i would tell him to stop pulling,
and he would reluctantly slow to walk beside me.
then, 50 feet later, i'd have to tell him again.
finally, my arm starting to stretch out in front for the umpteenth
time, i got exasperated....
"BIG! if you don't cut it out we are going to turn around and go
home."

that must have gotten thru,
because he dropped back immediately,
and stayed in his proper position.

big, little and i have been watching them work in the fields down
on ben's place.
the soybeans had been harvested a while back, and they'd been
spreading fertilizer the last couple of days.
now there was a tractor with a planter attached waiting in the
field.

"what do you reckon they're putting in, mr big; winter wheat?"
big just looked up at me and grinned.
(he knows sometimes you seem smarter if you don't say
anything)

as we passed the entrance to the fields, i noticed a 1/2 inch thick
ratchet extension lying in the road,
along with a couple of large washers.
i figured that they had been using their tools on one of the pieces
of farm equipment;
then forgot and left those items laying on the equipment.
so they had bounced off when it hit the bump going onto the
pavement.
i picked them up figuring i would put in ben's mailbox on the
way home.

big and i turned around after a little over a mile,
i was planning to do short out and backs until the rain started
(that way we could get home before we got soaked)

20

as we started back, we saw someone had arrived and was
prepping the tractor;
loading seed from a big truck into the planter.
big was fascinated by the sound of the auger moving seed thru a
chute, but he was careful to stay at my side.

when we got close, i saw it was someone i didn't know,
but when we reached the gate, i held up the ratchet extension.
the man grinned as wide as big does.
me and big walked on in, and i gave him the extension,
and told him; "there's a couple of washers in my pocket."

i gave him those and he thanked me;
"i been using these for a pin"
he put the washers over a hole where one of the planter arms
attached, then inserted the extension.
i could see that all the other arms were held in place by large
metal pins.
if there is one thing farmers are good at, it is improvising,

but me and big probably saved him some hassle.
just like removing fallen branches from the road,
spotting lost tools is a public service good runners perform in the
country.

"that a good dog?" the man asked.
"he's a sweetheart"
as if on cue, big stepped forward and bent his head down.
he got a scratching behind the ears for his trouble
and wagged his tail happily.

we walked on.
"i forgot to ask what he was planting" i told big
"i suppose it will give us something to wonder about."

about a half mile from home we started getting hit with scattered
raindrops.
"looks like we might be about finished mr big."
big didn't seem bothered, so i added;
"if it don't rain any harder than this, we'll just keep going."

it did rain harder than that.
so i unfastened the strap around my umbrella and told big;
"if someone would invent a dog umrella, we could walk in any
weather."

then i hit the button and the umbrella popped open.
big jumped a foot
"okay, if someone would invent a silent, slow motion, dog
umbrella."
big stayed even with me, but he moved as far away as he could
get, watching the umbrella suspiciously.

i'm glad it wasn't amy with the umbrella.
big might have had to kill it.

it rained harder and big started to hurry.
"big, if you'll get under the umbrella, at least you'll be part dry"
i tried to hold the umbrella where it would cover us both.
big liked the umbrella even less than he liked the rain
and he began towing me along pretty fast.

i no longer had to worry about big wanting to keep going when
we reached the driveway,
he was zeroed in on getting home.
and then the bottom fell out and the rain came down in torrents.

i thought about just letting big loose.
there was only a little over a quarter mile to go,
and i had no doubt he would head straight for the porch.
well, make that only a little doubt.
i wasn't anxious to get into a game of "catch me if you can" in the
pouring rain, so i held on

big was now in full tow mode
and i found myself going faster and faster.
"you know i can't run, big"
i said as i reached running speed.

of course, i wasn't really running,
all i had to do was pick my feet up and put them down quick
enough that i didn't get pulled onto my face.

22

i want to tell you, folks, figure out how to harness a big
and anyone could run a 3 minute mile.

we hit the porch like a runaway train.
big was dripping wet.
we keep a dog towel on the porch for just such occasions,
but it was soon soaked and big was still drenched,
so i opened the door & hollered for amy to bring another towel.
she came out & we kept drying him.

big loves getting toweled off & his expression was one of ecstacy.
finally we got him down to just damp & we sat on the step to talk.
big would sit in front of me, and scoot back between my legs as
far as he could go,
then lean back until he was looking up into my face.
then he'd move into the bigwich position between us.
then he'd repeat his version of lap-sitting in amy's lap.
it was a good way to spend a rainy morning for us and the big...

until he was sitting in amy's lap
and i heard a thunderclap of a fart.

i looked over and amy was sitting there with a surprised
expression on her face.
big was looking off at nothing in particular,
with his most innocent expression

i swear, if the dog could purse his lips, he'd have been whistling.
then he got up and walked away.

"BIG!, did you just fart on me and walk awa..."
amy's voice trailed off as her eyes began to water.
i was already mouth breathing,
knowing full well that a whiff of big fart would knock a buzzard
out of the air.

we all laughed (even big)
and then, noticing that the rain had stopped,
i put big's blue leash back on and we went out to get his
breakfast while amy went in to catch her breath and get ready
for the day.

life is good out on the farm.
especially when you have a coach big in charge.
every day brings its fresh surprises.

laz

## november 21, 2011
## big's rainy day

big hates rainy days.

he is stuck in the bigloo all day long.
he will sit there with one paw hanging over the doorstep
his head sitting on that paw
looking forlornly out at the rain.
it is a sad sight to see.

today was supposed to be a rainy day all day long,
so amy and i took pity on the big.
about 10, i went and brought him up on the porch to eat.
he was so happy!

but he had a problem eating.
he didn't start to eat for a long time,
because he was busy cuddling up and getting petted.
when he did eat, he'd eat a bite or two
then he had to come back & cuddle again.

he lap sat, he bigwiched, he even rolled over for belly rubs,
he had about an hour and a half of good quality time before amy
and i had to move on.

the weather didn't stick with the schedule,
and the rain stopped
(on radar i can see it looping just to our south)
big came out and was jumping around in the mud
wagging his tail and playing by himself
(he is frequently spied on thru the window)
but he can't lie in his favorite spots because it is too muddy...

this is a problem big can solve.
he got his blanket out of the bigloo
spread it out on the ground
and is lying on that.
(he needs to teach sophie & little how to "arrange" bedding)

problem is, when the rest of the rain comes
he won't think to put it back up.
(he is only a dog...)

looking at the radar,
there is a possibility that we'll have an hour gap.
and i didn't get my "run" in today either.

big is about to get a welcome surprise.
we're going to take a stab at doing a couple of miles before the
rain returns.
(i am going to put his blanket in the bigloo for him before we
leave)

i hope we can finish before it starts raining again.
my bad leg isn't recovered from the last time coach big decided i
*could* run...
with the proper tow motor.

laz

**november 22, 2011**
**how stupid are ultrarunners? ask big**

ok.
i admit i can't really run any more.
but the stupid is still going strong.

big and i were racing the rain this morning.

as of last night, the line of rain was predicted to arrive at noon.
when i got up this morning we were still good to go.
had to wait, of course, for amy to take the big guy for a couple of
miles of real running
so little and i put in a few to fill the time.
me and little ran over our allotted time,
so the big start was beginning to press the rain-free window.

i took one last look at the radar before we headed out.
looks good.
rain is moving SW to NE
along a front that was proceeding steadily eastward.
everything was timed for an arrival at something closer to 11.

i tried to pretend i didn't see a projection bulging out to the
south
which, if it continued to grow, would hit us from the south well
before the current line arrived from the east.
if you pretend you don't see it, it won't happen.

big and i discussed it.
we could do 5 miles and finish around 11.
that was the front end of the rain potential.
we decided it would be smart to cut it to 3.

when we got to the planned turnaround
big wasn't paying attention
and before i noticed his oversight
we were well on the way to the 5 mile turnaround.
dumb dog.

well, there was little choice but to go on to the 5 mile
turnaround...right?
i mean, we have a 3 mile turnaround, and a 5 mile turnaround.
we couldn't just do some unknown distance in the middle.

we talked about it some more as we walked on.
"we aren't idiots, big. first sign of rain we turn around...
no matter where we are."

"besides, we are moving at top speed now.
we'll finish before 11."

the cloud cover kept getting thicker and darker.
then we heard a long, rolling, rumble of thunder.
"that's our sign big, its time to turn around."
big just looked at me. he wasn't grinning.

"i know, i know, we can see the 5 mile turnaround from here,
but thats just because we are on a long straightaway."
big just looked at me. he still had that solemn look on his face.
"you're right, big. look how much farther we've already gone just
talking about it. lets put the hammer down."

we had to do an even distance.
admittedly, we don't keep logs.
(well, i don't. i haven't looked in the bigloo to see if big has one)
we aren't training for a race.
but how can you be a runner and just do some unknown
distance?
that's...
blasphemous.

so we pushed on to the 5 mile turnaround and started back.
for the longest time it looked like the gamble would pay off.

when we crossed back over the highway without seeing a single
raindrop i started to feel almost cocky.
"see big, i told you we had plenty of time."
i looked at my watch.
"dadgum, we'll be home by 10:45.
we are burning it up today mr big"

28

less than 100 yards further along i felt a fat raindrop splat on my
head. others began to plop on the pavement in front of us.
"we're ok, mr big. these are just scouts.
the main force will be way behind."
big looked a little dubious.
"20 minutes big. it just needs to hold off for 20 minutes and you'll
be snug in your bigloo."

as we crossed the low water bridge
(which will be under water in a few hours)
i told big;
"look at the bright side. at least we got back before the bridge
was underwater.
we'd have had to walked 4 or 5 more hours in the rain to get
home the long way."

big didn't seem to see the bright side.
he was focused on staying beside me & keeping up a steady pace.
the scattered sprinkles had grown to a full fledged rain.
i popped open my umbrella

big didn't even notice the umbrella this time.
after the other day he had figured out it was harmless.
besides, he was concentrating on getting us home.
"you can't pull me to the house today, big. my leg won't take that
again."

every step we took, it rained harder.

when we reached the pug's house the rain hitting the leaves
sounded like a rushing torrent.
lynnor's obnoxious little pug didn't bother to come out,
giving one cursory bark from the porch.
big didn't waste time on a pee-mail response either.

by the time we started up the drive, it was pouring down.
"you messed up today big fella. if you had listened to me and
turned around sooner we wouldn't have even got wet."

when we reached the porch, i let go of the leash
and big shot up the steps.

29

once on the porch, he shook off (spraying water on everything)
then he went and stood beside the dog towel.

"was that your plan mr big? get us soaked, just so you'll get
toweled off?"
big grinned.
big loves being toweled off almost as much as he hates getting
wet.

so now big is cozy and dry in his bigloo.
sleeping away a rainy afternoon isn't half bad if you get in your
workout first.

but it has to be whole miles....

right?

ultrarunners are not too bright.
and their coaches aren't making them smarter.

laz

## november 26, 2011
## big thanksgiving

this year marked a new milestone.
thanksgiving dinner was at our house.
once it was at the grandparents house.
then it was at the parents.
now it is here.

it just didn't seem right for thanksgiving to be a bad day for the
big when everyone else was going to have a fun day,
so i got up early to make sure he got a good long walk...

while amy was running with the big,
i took little for her turn.
it was a great morning.
cool, almost chilly with a thick fog.

little & i went down short creek
and made note of how cold the fog gets down in the bottoms.
we saw a nice 6-point buck
and walked within 50 feet of him before he spotted us.
i was hoping there were no hunters around.
i don't like to be that close to a target when idiots might be
carrying guns.

i was surprised that the fog was still so thick when big and i left,
but i was glad.
it made for an especially nice morning...
except worrying about hunters.
my orange hat doesn't stand out so good in the fog.

it was a feast of the senses.
the chill on my skin
the hush that seems to always descend in a fog
except for invisible birds singing,
as if the day were special for them as well.

the pastures covered with heavy dew
seemed to shimmer green in the bright but diffuse light.

31

cows would materialize from the fog and watch us walk past
just chewing and staring as cows are won't to do.
a large bull stared down big as we passed
i think he was considering if he should act as the protector of the
herd. he seemed relieved as we continued on past.

the winter wheat, now a sea of 4 inch sprouts
was like pale green shrouds on ben's fields.
and behind every scene, in the background
the forests were just dark shapes barely visible in the fog.
big and i discussed how lucky we were to be out there for such a
show
he must have been inspired
because he was particularly well mannered.

as we came to the 90 degree turn on millersburg
a small pickup truck emerged from the fog coming towards us.
we moved to the far lane to let him pass,
which put big on the truck's side
the driver started to make the turn wide,
until he saw us coming out of the fog.

then he cut it short in his own lane.
big always starts towards passing cars,
looking into the drivers window to see if it is someone he knows
maybe someone who'll pet him.
this must have been someone else heading to thanksgiving
dinner, because i didn't recognize the driver
and he had obviously never seen big before.

you have to be ready for big's curious look.
he sort of drops his head,
which raises a hump of muscle over his shoulders
which in turn emphasizes his linebacker neck
(it is as big around as his head and slopes down to his shoulders)
he pricks up his ears and squints his eyes
which makes his massive jaw muscles stand out.
his ears, which are actually on the sides of his skull,
look like they divide the wide top of his head into thirds.
his eyes, which are large and set wide apart
look small and close together.

they seem to be boring holes thru you,
yellow and unblinking
add in his short muzzle,
and he looks more like a devil bear than a dog.


it is a thoroughly intimidating look,
even when you know what it means.


this poor guy was driving thru the fog
when he had to slow down to make a sharp turn without hitting
us as we appeared out of nowhere.
for just a moment his face and big's were about 4 feet apart.
i guess i am not a very nice person,
but the expression on his face was priceless.
i think he half expected big to rip off his tires and disable the
truck so he could pull out the driver for breakfast.
i don't know if he even saw me at all.

"i don't think he'll be stopping to talk, mr big."
big looked up at me solemnly as if to say;
"i know. its not the first time."
and we walked on.


a little later we were walking with forest on both sides of the
road when some wild turkeys took off from their roost in a tree
and flew across the road over us.
"look big, a wild turkey...
no make that two... no three, four... five turkeys!"
a single flight feather came off the last turkey and spiraled to the
ground,
sticking, point first, right next to us.
i picked it up and stuck it in my orange hat
and we walked on.


a little later we passed a hunter sitting in his truck.
he was waiting on his buddy to come out of the woods.
he rolled down his window to say hello.
"beautiful morning ain't it?"
"sure is. its a great day to be out."
"is that the dog that runs with the girl?"
"yeah, thats him."

"bet she don't have no trouble."
"naw, he's pretty protective of her."
"he is sure a fine looking dog."
"thanks. i couldn't ask for a better companion."
by then we were a ways down the road, so we walked on.

the rest of the way was just your every day fine walk.
i stopped to look at the creeks.
big stopped to mark the biggest trees.
every time we came to an intersection,
big checked to see if we didn't need to go the longer way.
"naw, big. we need to go on home. we have to get back before
people start arriving."
"i know i've promised before, but one of these days we're gonna
walk all the way to fosterville & back."
big just looked at me. i don't know if he believes me or not.

we got home in plenty of time and got big fed,
but most of the rest of the day would be a disappointment for the
big guy.
people would come walking up to the door
and big would jump around in excitement,
his round face lit up with joy.
they would look at him and hurry into the house.
sometimes they would stop to pet little and sophie.
but no one wanted to visit the big.

he would look disappointed and go back to lie in the sun.
once in a while i would go out and be the consolation prize.
big always greeted me like this visit was the most exciting
minute of his life.
"they aren't ignoring you to be mean, big
it isn't personal.
you're sort of scary looking."
big would look up at me solemnly as if to say;
"i know. its not the first time."

case and lex came,
and they went out to visit big.
he loves his case and lex.

34

finally, the party broke up
and everyone went off to their homes.
i went out to feed big and freshen his water bowl.
after a few minutes of petting i told him, like i do every day;
"ok. mr big, its time."

he looked up at me with his happy face;
"it was a good thanksgiving."
big always focuses on what he gets, not what he doesn't get.
then he trundled off to his bigloo to sleep.

tomorrow will be a new day, full of fresh surprises.

laz

**november 28, 2011**
**the big storm**

thanksgiving evening, before everyone had left
we put up a tent over the dog pen.
sandra had one of those big 10x10 tents with sides
and we wanted to fix the pen so that sophie & little could have a
place to stay outside
even when it was rainy.
we had to erect the tent before we put it over the pen,
and we needed the extra muscle power from our younger guests
to lift the tent over the pen after we put it up.

this makes about the 10th time we have tried to rig up shelter
over the pen.
but there is a tradition that goes with these attempts.
as soon as we finish constructing the latest roof and walls
some monster storm hits and demolishes our work.

last night the storm came.
it blew chairs off the porch and hit the tent like a freight train.
the tent was severely battered,
the poles were bent, and several of the braces were snapped.
it was damaged, but still standing this morning.
i braced it up the best i could.
hopefully it will stand for a while, because it does still provide
some protection from the rain.

it had to be the biggest storm yet
because it snapped the ropes holding big's tarp
(and those had withstood two tornadoes!)

big had managed to stay dry inside the bigloo his friends
provided, but as soon as i came outside this morning
he came out into the rain and began barking for help.
he did not like his tarp being down and rain coming in through
his bigloo door.

i brought big up on the porch and amy and I dried him off.
his small blanket was in the doorway of the bigloo, and was wet

37

so i brought it up as well and hung it on one of the retrieved
chairs to dry.

then amy sat with big
while i went out into the rain to repair his tarp.
i already had some heavier duty ropes for when this day came.
as could be expected, it was pure fun rehanging the tarp in the
rain.
amy tried to help by repeatedly asking me from the porch if i
wasn't done yet.
"of course not. i am screwing around so i can be out here in the
rain as long as possible."

when i got to the part where i was trying to attach the ropes and
tie them up in trees, the heavy swearing started.
there is scant comfort in having read the mathematical equations
that explain why ropes and strings always tangle.
(and that is without tree branches and other obstacles to
contribute)
once the heavy swearing began, amy chose to visit quietly with
big and not offer any further encouragement.

after i finished, he had a nice setup.
improved over the original tarp.
but the ground around his bigloo was already pure mud
that won't go away until the whole yard dries out again.

with the forecast calling for another 48 hours of rain
no one was going to be taking big running today.
and i was soaked thru.
thanksgiving i had planned to build a fire in the porch fireplace
but no one had been enthusiastic about it
(probably because it was about 75 degrees)
so i already had wood piled up.

i decided to build that fire
so me and big could spend a cold rainy morning on the porch
sitting by a warm fire
(and i could dry out).
big loved it. and the fire was so inviting that amy and sandra both
came outside.

38

big ate.
we made a bigwich with amy's help (at big's insistence)
and later while amy was inside showering he rolled over for
some belly rubs.
big started working sandra while she sat by the fire.
he looked into her eyes and wagged his tail
then he lay down at her feet.
he is a clever boy. charming the ladies, but never too pushy.

i decided this was a good time for one of his giant chew toys.
i got one of those huge rawhide bones with a knot at each end.
that ought to take big all day...

he bit the ends off and ate the middle in about 5 minutes.
it took another 5 to consume one of the knots.
then he took the last knot and started to walk around the porch...
looking.

he was trying to find a place to hide his prize.
he checked around in the corner behind the fireplace
scratching around in a box of junk and poking around to see if
there was something he could put his bone under.

he looked at what was left of the firewood stack,
but most of the wood had already gone into the fire.
he stood up tall and looked into the garbage can
but it was empty.

he looked off the porch down into the flower beds, but i told him;
"don't even think about it, big.
he looked at me,
then he moved on to my shoes.

i leave my muddy boots on the porch when i am inside
and when i come out i take off my houseshoes, put on the boots,
and leave the houseshoes on the porch.
i was still wearing the boots
and my houseshoes must have looked like the perfect place,
because he looked onto the foot hole,
and leaned over to drop his rawhide knot into my shoe;
"no, not my shoes big!"

big looked at me & moved on...

the only place left was the storage bag the tent had come in.
it was laying on the porch next to my shoes.
big set his bone on top
and started scratching at it to turn it over on top of the bone.

i went over and got the bone,
lifted a corner of the bag and put the bone under it.
big gave a look of satisfaction,
and started to come join us again
when he noticed little and sophie (who had been asleep in the
house) looking out the window at him.

he gave them a look that clearly said;
"damnation."

then he went back and got his bone out of its hiding place...
and started searching again.
feeling sorry for the big guy, i said;
"here you go big, i'll take care of it for you."
and held out my hand.
big gave me his treat and i put it up on my work table.
big sniffed at the table, then went over and laid back down by
sandra.

in just a moment, big got back up.
he went over to the jug i use to fill his water bowl,
looked at the jug, then looked at me.

i got the spare water bowl we have on the porch and filled it up.
big took a big drink
(rawhide chews must work up a big thirst)
then he went and looked at his blanket hanging on the chair.
then he looked at me.
i checked it and it was fairly dry, so i picked it up.
big went and stood next to sandra.
so i put his blanket there beside her and big settled in with a sigh.

i think sandra was duly impressed.

i don't know if she quite believed the stories me and amy tell
about big.
but that was because she'd never seen him in action before.

eventually amy had to go to work.
then later on sandra had to go.
finally, when everything was about dried out
and the fire was getting low.
i took big and his blanket back out to his bigloo.
he went in, turned and stuck his head back out for one last
scratch behind the ears.
that taken care of, he went in and laid down to nap away the rest
of the rainy day.

i think we all had a nice rainy morning.
talking around the fire like people used to do before cell phones
and computers.
i'm glad we had a big storm last night.
and i'm glad we have a big.

laz

## november 28, 2011
## I didn't promise big I wouldn't tell

we did the fire on the porch thing with big again today.

after a while amy said;
"my dog likes to sit by the fire, too...
why can't my dog come sit by the fire?"

i just shrugged.

so amy went and got sophie and brought her out on the porch.
big came running to greet her, he was so ready to play.
sophie rolled onto her back.
big jumped around trying to coax sophie into getting up.
finally he accidentally stepped on her and sophie yelped.

i called big over to me to lessen sophie's fear
amy said;
"come on over here by the fire, sophie."
and pulled her on her leash to get her to come over to the fire.

we have a new term here now;
the "sophie belly crawl"

sophie "walked" to the fire with her belly scraping the ground,
watching big out of the corner of her eye.
i was laughing so hard that my stomach hurt.
even amy was laughing.

after sophie had been groveling in front of the fire for a while,
watching big with a look of terror
amy saw that sophie was not going to really enjoy her time on
the porch with big, and said;
"ok sophie, lets go inside."

sophie bellycrawled all the way to the door with one eye still on
the big.
once inside, she almost ran to her dog bed,
from which she has not budged since...

we are looking for advice on how amy can train sophie to be less
aggressive.

little came busting out while the door was open.
we already know why big and little can't share time on the porch
by the fire.
when big and little get together they are going to play, period.
they cannot play in a confined space.

laz (still wiping the tears from my eyes)

## november 29, 2011
## big and the first snow

we got our first snow of the year today.
some of you might not consider it snow,
there was only accumulation on roofs and car tops.
but snow was falling from the sky instead of rain...
mostly.
around these parts we take any snow we can get.

coach big and i hadn't been out in two days,
except a hurried mile during a slack period in the rain yesterday.
coach big and amy hadn't been out at all in two days.

coach big does not believe in days off...
or stress injuries, or fatigue, or any other reason for missing a
workout.
big was rarin to rip.

amy and big went first, knocking out a 3 miler that i hoped would
take a little of the edge off big.

it didn't.
big was at full strength for our walk.

we left in tiny, almost microscopic snow.
i was wearing my thermal work gloves, hoping to avoid cold
fingers.
we left into the wind.
i always like to face the wind on the way out.
otherwise, when it shifts at the halfway mark
it won't be in your face on the way home.
big always like to walk head on into a cold wind.
he thinks it feels great!

the snow stopped by the time we got to the road,
and i was a little disappointed.
but there was still a decent headwind.
sure enough, thermal gloves or no thermal gloves,
my fingers got cold.

45

but after 2 days in the house,
me & coach big were glad to be out.
we were moving at a pretty good clip,
except big had to refresh a lot of course markings as we went.

once we reach the road we can see the hills.
it was a misty morning, with banks of fog drifting up little valleys
and emerging from the trees over streams and springs.
the freeze line was about 200 feet above the valley we were
walking, so the tops of all the hills were white,
as if they were wearing shawls against the cold of the fog.

about 20 minutes out, it started a misting rain.
by then we were warmed up and feeling good.
my fingers were no longer cold.

it is like a fresh surprise every time
when my fingers start out getting cold,
i worry it will be miserable
and then they warm up once i get going and i feel great.

big and i had decided to do the short stretch of highway between
the ends of short creek loop.
we'd been saving it for a day when we didn't want to range too
far. given the possibility of real rain, i wasn't anxious to get too
far from home.

big loves to do new roads as much as i do.
even familiar roads that have been driven often
withhold many of their secrets,
for the foot traveler to discover.

the misting rain turned to tiny ice pellets.
i could see them bouncing off big's wide back.
we were walking with woods on either side of the road
and the ice hitting the leaf litter made a sound like a distant
waterfall.

the highway passed thru a cut where a finger of low ridge
crossed the roadway.
looking at the rock on either side

46

i marveled at the many small seams and fissures,
exposed when the rock was cut thru like the roots of an upside
down tree, they wind and twist thru the rock face and gather
together into larger cracks before descending into the ground.
those are what carry the groundwater down to the underground
streams.

if we were in a car, this would pass in a second,
and i wouldn't get to see any of it.

when we reached the other end of short creek loop
the ice had turned to genuine snowflakes.
it would be better if the ground was white
(better still if the snow was a foot or two deep)
but it is always magical to "run" in the falling snow.
the flakes were slipping off big's back,
or sticking for a few moments before vanishing.

our plans kept changing with the precipitation.
when it snowed or iced,
we were going to do another loop on the other side of the house.
when it was raining, we were going to stop at the house.

we stopped at the bridge to watch short creek rushing past.
earlier the bridge had been underwater
and the roiling surface was still less than a foot beneath us.
when we reached the driveway we were getting a fairly steady
rain.
but instead of going straight to the house
we went on out to the overlook at the end of the winston's
driveway.
the white capped hills and the foggy valley were a view worth a
little extra rain.

then we headed to the house.

ok, i know this wasn't much of a snow.
this was just a teaser.
i can't wait until the big fella takes me out into a real snow.

laz

**december 07, 2011**
**big or medium?**

well, the cable just weighed in on the debate.

amy and sophie were out on sophie's run,
when amy heard this sound coming down the road....
"DADARUMP-DADARUMP-DADARUMP"
it was big,
thundering down the road like a runaway train,
about a foot of cable hanging lifeless from his neck.

his "160 pound dog" cable had snapped
(big says it is amy's fault for walking the inferior dog first!)

we have him (very) temporarily on little's cable
but that is only meant for a dog of big's measured weight
so i know it won't last long at all.

i will take him out for his walk,
after which he has a nap on the schedule...
and big keeps to his schedule.

that will give me time to go see if they have a stronger cable.
at least the old one should still be under warranty?
it hasn't begun to weather yet.

i just have this feeling the salesman is going to look at that frayed
cable end
then look at me over the top of his glasses and say;
"did you try to contain a big with this cable?"

"it isn't guaranteed to hold a big. nothing will hold a big for long."

laz

**december 07, 2011**
**big or medium (part 2)**

took the cable back to a very puzzled pet store.
seems no dog had ever broken one of their cables before.
particularly an 80 pound dog on a 160 pound dog cable.

now big has a 250 pound cable.
i was going to wait until supper to take it out
(he is peacefully asleep in the bigloo)
but it is snowing to beat 60.
we might have to do an extra walk today.

laz

**december 12, 2011**
**did big and i see cranes today?**

big and i were out on the big trail this morning,
putting in our miles,
when we heard an unfamiliar sound.

it was a sort of trilling/warbling call.
big and i were discussing what it might be
when a flock of 10-12 big birds came into sight.

they were pretty high up,
but the general appearance reminded me of the local herons
except i have never seen the herons in groups, only solitary.
herons are also blue/blue gray,
and these birds looked more gray or white
(they were in a bright sun, so it was hard to tell)
they might even have been tan colored.
and i haven't ever hear a heron make a sound like that.

the pattern of calling was remniscent of the migrating geese that
pass over,
and these birds seemed to be moving south with purpose.
so big suggested maybe these were sandhill cranes
(or heck, whoopers for all we know)

i know there are some bird experts on the list.
did we possibly have a crane sighting this morning?
(big is curious about stuff like that)

laz

**december 16, 2011**
**bigsprints**

this has not been a great fall for the big.
since the start of november it has rained, and rained, and rained
some more.
big does not like rain.
he doesn't like getting rained on
and he does not like staying in the bigloo all day.

i have done everything i could to reduce the unpleasantness.
we have played the radar like a roulette wheel,
rushing out to get in miles between fronts.
more than once we have lost the gamble and got soaked.

big has the routine down.
we get home in the rain and head for the porch.
he makes a beeline for the dog towels to get dried off.
big does love to be toweled down,
almost enough to make it worth getting rained on.

on unbroken rainy days we spend his normal walking time on
the back porch.
big likes porch time.
he can sit on my feet and lean back against me.
there is head patting, ear rubbing, neck stroking, and chest
scratching...

when he feels like it, there is even food to eat.
sometimes there are new toys...
rawhide chews with a life expectancy measured in seconds
or bones whose life span can stretch into minutes.

it only takes seeing him crush a hambone in his jaws once to
understand why people are not always anxious to pet his huge
head...

or why the guys down the road quit slowing their pickup trucks
down to flirt when amy started running with the big.

55

the only thing about porch time is,
there is no exercise.
small spaces do not lend themselves to big play.

but this is the big.
the dog who invents his own tricks.
and he has come up with a game that we can play on the porch.
we call it bigsprints.

this morning we caught a gap in the rain and squeezed in a fast
mile. then we retreated to the back porch for some quality time.
after spending a while petting and talking
and eating a decent breakfast
big got to prancing around with a gleam in his eye.
there is no missing it when big feels like playing.

amy had come out to pet the big,
she hadn't seen big doing his bigsprints on the porch,
altho she has heard about them
so i told her to stay on the back step
(so she wouldn't get trampled)
and i went down to the other end by the fireplace.
then i leaned over and slapped my knees.
big gave a little start, looking at me with his eyes wide.
"go-go-go-go-go-go"

big tucked his butt and took off.
now the back porch is only 40 feet long and 10 feet wide.
one lengthwise side is the wall of the house,
the other is a 5 foot dropoff into flowerbeds
one end is the fireplace,
the other is a 5 foot dropoff into flowerbeds.
big can hit top speed on the straightaways
corner like a tetherball
and stop on a dime.
the butt-tucked position gives him incredible power, acceleration
and manueverability.

it also gives him the appearance of a red, hairy wrecking ball
with an ear to ear grin.
he comes thundering towards you,

56

looking like he will fly off into space,
crash into the fireplace
(or knock you into next week)
and instead executes a 180
and rockets back off the way he came.

if i am standing in the middle of the porch,
he will leap into the air as he goes past,
flashing in front of my face like a red grinning cannonball
he zips between table legs and flys around chairs
and never touches anything.

then he will come flying straight at you
and at the last second just stop dead in his tracks,
panting and looking at you with laughter in his eyes.

this is a game, and games require more than one player.
you are supposed to slap your hands on your knees and call the
next round;
"go-go-go-go-go-go-go"
then the big can tuck that butt and blast off again.

big had a rare floor mistake today.
ok, maybe it was really my fault.
or maybe it wasn't a floor mistake,
but a necessary adjustment to make a particularly difficult turn.

he was making his south end 180's between the fireplace hearth
and a chair
(in a space with about an inch of clearance on either side)
and i stepped into the path where he would be coming out of his
next 180, forcing him to instead make a 270 into an immediate
reverse 90...

it was too much centrifugal force, even for the big
his rear end slipped just a little coming out of the 270
and his hip banged off my shin
(it felt like he broke my tibia)

or maybe he just used my shin for leverage to execute the
reverse direction 90...

57

because he nailed that one.

no big game is complete until i am injured and swearing,
amy is laughing at me
and big is laughing with pure joy.

bigsprints don't last a long time.
the energy demand is enormous.
it wasn't too long before a pooped big was ready to head for the
bigloo and take a nap.

he'd much rather lie in the sun,
but it has not been a great fall for the big.

on the other hand, it could be worse.
big has a way of squeezing out all the fun that is possible,
regardless of the situation.

laz

## december 20, 2011
## big meets santa

big and i had yet another race with the rain this morning,
checking the radar and guessing how much time we had.
the last couple of times we have mis-estimated and finished up wet.
this morning we nailed it so well that the first drops started to
fall as we passed the back porch on the way back to the bigloo.

i was worried that big would pull me along
since he didn't get to run with amy this morning.
amy is trying to claim food poisoning
(just because i cooked supper last night)

i tried to reason with her,
i ate the same food and had no problems at all.
amy's response was that i was immune to food poisoning.
what can i say.
if she wasn't such a princess & ate food out of the garbage now
and then, or maybe consumed something the dog had chewed on
once in a while, she wouldn't be so fragile.

i am cooking again tonight.
i'll have to fix something gentle for her upset tummy.
i am thinking maybe a sharp cheddar and sausage, habanero
omelot.
that would settle anyone's stomach.

anyway, despite my concern,
big was in excellent form this morning.
psychic, as always, he didn't bark for amy to come out and run as
he does every other morning
(she says it is because he heard her throwing up all night)

instead he greeted me with an enthusiastic *wooo-wooo-wooo* and
performed a couple of extra flips.
then he was a real gentleman during the walk
which makes it a lot more enjoyable for me.
we did the broiles road 5 mile loop this morning,

59

which has both the trailer dogs and the goat corner dog.
and we ran into mr winston's new dog,
which has become a real nuisance lately.
this morning the little nuisance got within 6 inches of dog trainer
range.
one more step, and he's going to get a lesson he won't soon
forget.
its coming soon.
thru it all, big stayed on task like a pro.

the only incident came when we ran into santa.
big don't care much for santa.

as we were approaching the last farm before the short creek
church, big started hanging back a little.
i asked him what was up,
and he kind of slid in behind me, peeking around my legs.
i looked up ahead, and there was santa.

the folks in the last farm had hung a life-size inflatable santa
figure from their gate.
and what a santa it was.
he wasn't roly poly fat, he was built like big.
he looked more schwartzenegger than clause.

he did have on the standard red suit and hat,
but in place of a jolly laughing face,
this santa had more of a grimacing sneer.
this was the kind of santa that sends small children running to
their mothers, screaming in fear.

and if that wasn't enough,
the pre-rain wind had kicked up,
and santa was waving his arms,
warning us to keep our distance.

nope. big did not care for santa at all.
as we passed the menacing figure
big's assigned position on the left would have him passing closest
to santa.
big wanted none of that.

as we got closer, you could see that santa wasn't just threatening us by waving his arms, he was jerking and pulling against the ropes tying him to the gate, no doubt trying to pull loose so he could come after us.

big ignored the proscription against crossing in front or behind me. it didn't matter if he got scolded, or not;
he definitely wanted me between him and this strange demon santa from hell.
santa just leered at us, and continued straining at his bonds and waving his arms.

once we were past
big moved to the front and walked along looking over his shoulder. i could have walked him into a telephone pole or off the bridge into short creek with no problem.

big continued to look over his shoulder periodically
even after santa was long out of sight.

nope. big don't care much for santa.

laz

## december 23, 2011
## big superball

the winter of rain continues.
big is the only one lucky that i am unemployed
(if he couldn't buy his own food, he wouldn't be so lucky)
otherwise he'd have been trapped in his bigloo a lot.

this morning we had another successful rain-race
(even without the big rain app)
i knew it was coming, so i got up early
and we got in 2 miles before the first showers hit.
we got an extra treat on the way home,
the sun was rising behind the clouds
and they were streaked with glowing red
like a bank of hot coals in the sky.

then we spent some quality time on the porch
before the poor big fella had to return to his bigloo
to sleep thru another cold rainy day.

this afternoon i brought him up for a round of bigsprints before
supper.
having him racing around the porch is like being in a handball
court with a 90 pound superball being shot from a cannon.

big taught me a couple of new games.
there was "can that dog jump?"
i hold my hand out high, and ask;
"can that dog jump?"
then big leaps into the air, trying to touch my hand with his nose
and i exclaim;
"YES, that dog can jump!"
big's eyes just twinkle with laughter.

the other game wasn't so easy.
as he raced past me doing his bigsprints,
and leaped high as he passed
big decided it would be funny to turn his head and punch me in
the chest with his nose.

63

the first one was a surprise
the second one was funny
the third one thumped into my sternum like a fastball.
it rocked me pretty good.
i had to tell him to be careful.
after that he just tried to touch my chest with his nose.

it didn't take long to burn off a lot of big energy
and after supper was served and a bone
(which he crunched into slivers and ate in about 2 minutes)
he was content to go back out to the bigloo as it was getting dark.

right now he is a sad big.
chrys came home for the holidays.
he was fine until he heard her speak to me on the porch.
after that he started barking for her to come and say hello.
he hadn't seen her in a month
when she didn't come to see him;
"it is dark and cold and muddy!"
he cried for a little bit.

that big ugly dog has tender feelings.
it will all be forgotten in the morning...
as soon as he gets to give her a proper greeting.
when we start our walk
you can bet the farm he'll be wanting to come up on the porch
and look in the back door to see where chrys is.

chrys better not plan on sleeping in.

laz

**january 01, 2012**
**little things make a big difference**

big's internet friends have been really good to him.

he had been having a rotten fall, due to all the rain.
even when he wasn't trapped in the bigloo all day because of the
rain, the ground was so wet he couldn't do his favorite thing;
lay in the sun and sleep.

shortly before christmas, big got a package in the mail...

his own sleeping platform.
(amy calls it his chaise lounge)
the rain and mud continue to plague us,
but as i write, there is one contented big
laying on the big lounge chair in the sun.

it requires a little extra work.
in the summer his area is mostly in the sun all day.
currently, with the sun at its southernmost,
he only has a patch of sun.
his sunny patch travels across his area really fast.
so every hour or two i have to go relocate his chair.
(he'll probably figure out how to do it himself sooner or later)

he doesn't mind at all.
he has discovered another use for the big lounge.
it makes a perfect platform for rolling on his back for a belly rub.

sometimes it is good to be a big.

laz

**january 06, 2012**
**you're making a big mistake**

i love to spy on big in the morning.
most mornings he runs with amy first.
i have time to walk with him later, and he loves his runs.
i wouldn't want him to miss his opportunity to run while we are
out walking.

it doesn't matter what time we get up,
since big hears our eyes open, he is already waiting before we
can look...
unless it is raining.
he doesn't care how cold it is, he will be waiting.
but he knows we don't go out in the rain.
on rainy days he can sleep in.

big starts his day by going to the very end of his cable
as close as he can get to the back porch
(where amy comes out)
then he turns backwards and lays down with his butt facing the
porch.
that gets him a body length closer.
as a finishing touch, he sticks out one hind leg
getting just that much closer.
then he watches the window for any humans moving in the
house.

when i first go downstairs in the morning i always look
and there he is, butt to the house, head on his paws,
one hind leg stuck out.
waiting.

i love to spy on him when amy goes out with sophie.
as soon as the door handle turns big leaps to his feet,
and turns to face the porch, tail wagging expectantly.
then he sees amy with sophie on a leash.
he gets a look of pure astonishment on his face
and starts to bark furiously,
warning amy that she is making a BIG mistake!

67

it doesn't matter that it happens every day,
he still cannot believe that amy is running with the inferior dog.

he will keep trying to warn her until she is finally out of hearing...
his hearing, which extends for a long way.

when she gets within a quarter mile of the house on her return
trip, he starts barking again.
he is so relieved that she has miraculously survived,
with no better protection than sophie.
and he keeps it up until she finally comes back out to get a REAL
dog.
he leaps and does flips until she reaches him and tells him to SIT
which he knows he has to do, if there is to be a run.

then they are off.
big with his wide eyes and huge grin
totally focused on the task at hand...
which is to show her how it is to run with a REAL dog.
surely tomorrow she won't risk her life by running with that
inferior dog.

once they get back
big will start barking for me.
there is still work to be done.
me and big patrol all those places that amy never goes,
the whole territory needs to be monitored,
and all the markings need to be kept fresh,
so everyone will know when they come to BIG'S ROAD.

if i don't come right away,
big will resume the waiting position,
butt to the porch, one hind leg stuck out.
but he doesn't just wait patiently.
like a snooze alarm, every 5 minutes he gets up and barks a
reminder.
there is important work to be done.

it is tough being a big.
there is important work to be done,
and no one seems to realize the urgency.

68

amy needs to be watched over,
and she foolishly risks everything by going out with a broomstick
of a half-dog.
big has to worry and worry.

but we do finally get everything attended to...
probably thanks to big staying on top of it all.
then it is time to have a hearty breakfast
and lay in the sun on the big chaise lounge....

resting up for tomorrow morning,
when he will have to start the whole process again.

a big's work is never done.

laz

## january 07, 2012
## BIG

> Why in God's name do you make that wonderful dog
> live outside chained up by the neck?
>        Bruce

you say that as if i were in charge!

big can't stay in the house...

number one is sandra's prized hardwood floors and big's huge claws.
this is a dog who sometimes just gets a whim and jumps up to look me in the eye...
and does flips... not to mention bigsprints.

number two is big's size and strength...
and enthusiasm.
a tornado would make a better housepet.

number three is big would want the thermostat set at no higher than 40. i have seen him sunbathing at 20.
once he figured out the thermostat he would freeze us all to death.

number four is big understands refrigerators.
tony had to put a padlock on his.
in nashville, they could not leave him in the house unattended.
(although he does have the manners to shut the door after he picks out a snack)

number five is that big can open doors. he can use the handle, but if it is locked he can take it off the hinges.
big thinks all doors should be open.
and yes, he believes that all pet doors fit him... and they will.

number six is that big does not believe in curtains.
he believes windows are exclusively to look out.

to his credit, he doesn't destroy curtains.
he just takes them down.

number seven is the storage cabinet mystery. while he was at
tony's there was a picture going around.
it was called, "where is the dog?"
you can see one side of a room, with a row of some sort of
partitioned shelf or storage cabinets along the ceiling...
about 8 feet high.

at first you cannot see a dog, then you notice this bowling ball
sized head grinning out of the center cabinet.
about 8 feet in the air.
my first question was; "how the heck did he get up there?"
the answer, of course; "we don't know."

number eight is sandra's prized hardwood floors.
i want to live.

big will not stay in a pen. any pen.
he can jump, he can dig.
and when we built him a doggie gulag,
with 6 foot chain link fence walls and a stone floor
we found out he knows how to unravel chain link.

big likes his cable.
i have read all the terrible stuff about chaining dogs
but that is how big likes to be kept. he can see all around him
(and foolish small animals can try to walk across his space)

the other day he had taken off his cable...
the old 160 pound cable had a complex latch that took both
hands to fasten or unfasten
he was only able to take it off a couple of times.
but he snapped that cable,
and his new 200 pound cable has one of those simple latches that
you can open with your thumb.
that won't be much of a challenge for the big.
so sandra came home and big came around to meet her.
he sat beside the car looking at her while she texted me that he
was free...

i dont know why she texted me,
because i have no idea how to read a text on my cell phone.
she might as well have written it on a scrap of toilet paper, stuck
the note in an old sock, and buried it in the woods.

she could have sent me a voice mail, i suppose.
because i can't figure out how to listen to those either.
i only have a cell phone so i can give the number to potential
employers.
i can dial numbers to place calls and answer it if it rings.
that is all. as soon as i get a job i am discarding the damn thing.

but i digress.
sandra went in the house
so big came around to the back door to look in at her.
sandra went out and he led her to his cable so she could hook
him back up.
he must have had some business to attend to,
so he took the cable off
and then he couldnt put it back on by himself...

stupid dog.

laz

**january 08, 2012**
**team big**

once you are on team big, you can never leave.

our neighbor, dale, has been walking a lot
(neighbor being anyone living in the general short creek area)
he wants to walk a half-marathon with his daughter this spring.
he has been walking a lot of big's roads

altho we hadn't yet run into him while on patrol,
i am sure that big knows he has been there.
dogs see much of the world with their nose.
and when you see with your nose,
you can see not only what is there, but what was there.

one cool crisp morning big and i were out on a walk
just fixing to head out fosterville road,
when i heard a whistle,
one of those loud country whistles that skilled whistlers can use
to summon cows...
or kids.

my dad could whistle like that.
when he whistled, you could hear it for miles.
it was a command that could not be ignored.
usually it meant;
"time for supper. if you want your share you better be here to
claim it!"
when i heard that whistle,
i stopped whatever i was doing and ran home as fast as i could
go.

the decades have not erased the programming to respond to a
whistle so i looked around.
far behind us, i could see a small figure walking in our direction.
"what do you think, big, was that whistle for us?"
big looked at me for a moment, then he looked up the road;
"you know we have important work to do."

"yes, i know we have work to do. i think it might be dale, big. it
isn't ben, ben runs. i dont know who else it could be. dale might
want to walk with us."
big reluctantly waited. he didnt have a lot of choice.
i have lost a lot of excess weight on the big training program,
but, unlike amy, i still have plenty enough ballast to anchor a big.

it was indeed dale. he lives near the beginning of fosterville road,
and was just finishing up his morning walk.
with very little persuasion, he decided he would walk with us.
it was only 2 more miles to our turnaround.
not everyone has bigs and littles to keep them company on their
walks and runs, so traveling with someone else along is a treat.

big was a little leery at first.
until dale put down his stick.
big can't really relax around a man with a stick.
dale didn't need his stick for this part of his morning walk.
we have a big.

big likes to have someone along on our walks,
but he is a little skittish in the beginning
and if they walk in front of him, he pulls like a tractor.
big feels he needs to be in front,
except when we are doing "heel."

the walk soon settled in,
big making note of even the smallest change since our previous
patrol on fosterville road,
dale and i walking along and talking.
big was probably glad to have me talking to dale.
it kept me from distracting him from spotting everything new.
if there is so much as a bottle in the ditch,
or stick on the pavement,
it has to be noted.
this is big's road.
talking with me tends to be a distraction.

everything went great, until we got back where we started.
big welcomes new members on the team.

76

we are a powerful pack. we have big. we have a master who does
not even fear bicycles.
it is natural we should attract new members.

when we got back to the start of fosterville road,
we talked a moment, then dale picked up his stick and started
down liberty pike towards his house.

big became very anxious.
weren't we going to go that way?
we walk that way sometimes.
as the two roads angled away from each other,
we could look across a hayfield
and see dale's dwindling figure thru breaks in the trees along
liberty pike.

big kept looking at dale, and looking back at me.
"he is lost!"
"no, big. we can't take him home."
big was clearly unconvinced.

even after dale had gone out of sight up his driveway,
and we had turned up our own road,
big kept looking over his shoulder.

the next time we see dale, big will greet him as a long lost friend.
because, once you are on team big, you are on team big for life.

laz

## January 09, 2012
## Cow Miles

so amy wants to know if chasing cows counts as junk miles?

she had left for work
and a few minutes later she called to tell me one of mr winston's
cows was out in the road.
"what should i do?"

i asked if she could tell where it got out.
"no, it is just standing by the road eating grass."
i told her that i normally just chased them back in the main gate,
but the winstons have been out of town and the gate is locked.
and i wasnt sure how to contact whoever was watching the cows
while they were gone.

i pointed out that usually,
if you just chase them,
they'll go back the way they got out.

the next part of the conversation was like that blair witch movie.
i could hear amy hollering at the cow and breathing hard
along with running sounds.

after a couple of minutes she came back on the line;
"how do you get a cow to go where you want it?"
i had to think about that one.
i've been herding cows since i was a kid
and never really thought of it as an acquired skill.

the easy answer was to go the direction you want to go,
and give the feeding call.
cows always come for supper.
but i don't know what call mr winston uses.

the other answer was to circle wide
and approach them from the opposite direction you want them
to go, and yell and wave your arms.

while i was pondering how to articulate this amy said;
"wait, someone is here."
i heard a male voice saying something indistinguishable
then we returned to the blair witch effects.

this time, where-ever amy put the phone,
i could not only hear the heavy breathing and crashing thru the
bushes sounds,
i could hear her heartbeat.
judging from the heart sounds, she was getting a solid workout.
these fancy new phones are amazing.

finally she came back on and said,
"now i know how to make them go where you want. you just
point that way and go 'HUT, HUT'"
so now i know mr winston's feeding call.
my grandfather's call sounded like "whoooo come own cows"
my dad whistled.

she didn't know who had come,
but he had a key to mr winston's gate,
and let the cow back in.

amy had two comments about the experience.
"i never had this happen in nashville"
and
"does chasing cows count as training miles?"

well, i put it to the experts...

does it?

laz

## january 12, 2012
## the big bacon incident

big and i continued our hide and seek with the rain this morning.
last night, according to the weather report,
middle tennessee got about 2.5 inches of rain.
i think it was a lot more here.

spotting a break in the rain on the radar
big and i headed out
(umbrella in hand)
about 8 this morning.
big had been out calling me to arms since the rain started to
slack off an hour earlier.

we started by walking down to short creek
to see what the situation was with the bridge.

i could hear the waterfall going over the bridge long before we
got near and with my height advantage i could see the water
rushing over in a torrent long before big could see the bridge at
all.
"you're gonna be ready to turn around in just a minute, mr big"

i underestimated the big.
as we approached the edge of the water rushing over the bridge
i could see debris more than waist high in the trees alongside the
road. this had been one of the biggest floods since we lived out
here. big slabs of pavement, that had been removed from the
roadway by the flood, were washed up against the bridge
guardrails. out in the middle of the bridge, the rampaging water
was a little over knee deep.

i walked to the edge of the water and stopped.
big waded on out until he felt the leash get taut.
then he turned and looked at me;
"well? come on. lets go."
"mr big, the bridge is underwater."
"this is not where we turn around."
"we aren't crossing that, big guy"

81

big reluctantly came back,
altho, when he thought i was hesitating, he started out again,
but we did get turned around.

so then we walked a few miles the other way
keeping one eye on the sky.
we got to the furthest safe turnaround,
and seeing darker clouds were starting to show up in the south,
we headed for the house.

on the way back, i could see mr big was staring intently at
something up ahead in the road.
as we got closer i saw what had his attention.
there was a slice of bacon laying in the middle of our lane.

me and big are both thinkers.
we wonder about the mysteries of life.

i was thinking;
"why in the heck would someone throw a slice of bacon out of
their car?"

big was thinking;
"how can i get that slice of bacon into my mouth?"

i was wondering;
"did someone make a special trip out here to throw out that slice
of bacon, or was it just an impulse that came over them as they
were passing thru?"

big was wondering;
"how close to that slice of bacon can i get, without it being an
illegal formation?"

we could both see that the bacon was going to pass by on my
right.
big's place is on my left.
crossing in front is illegal.
i was watching big
big was watching the bacon.

82

as he came parallel to the bacon,
big dipped his front end down low,
reached out as far as he could reach with his paw
and deftly tried to scoop the bacon over to where he could get it.

he came up inches short. the bacon was too far away.

big kept walking, looking back at the bacon with a mournful
expression on that wide face.

i stopped, so big stopped and looked back up me.

"you really want that bacon, don't you big?"
big wagged his tail and licked his chops.
sandra always gets on to me for talking to that dog like he was a
person.
i would stop if he didn't act like he understood.

as soon as i picked up the bacon, big sat...
and licked his chops again.
i dangled the bacon in front of his nose;
"you know you have to wait, don't you big fella?"
big's eyes were on me, but his nose was undressing the bacon.

"okay, big"
big delicately snatched the bacon from my fingers
and gobbled it down with a look of ecstacy.
"that was almost obscene, big guy."
big looked up at me innocently.
"you been thinking about that bacon since we passed it on the
way out, havent you?"
big didn't give away any secrets, but i know about that nose of
his.

the rest of the walk was pretty uneventful,
after we got home and had his real breakfast
big had a little while before the rain returned
to lie on his chaise lounge
and dream that the bacon vandals will be back.

laz

83

## january 16, 2012
## big and the tree maze

we spy on big thru sandra's office window.
it is the only vantage point where we can see him
and he can't see us.

he can see you if you sit at the desk,
or look out the window.
but when we stay back in the shadows and peek around the corner
he can't see us.

i think he knows we are there anyway,
because he will stare intently at the window.
but he can't see us.

by spying thru the window we find out a lot of his secrets.
that's where we saw his technique for escaping the harness
and other amazing big tricks.

the other day, he was sleeping peacefully in the sun on his chaise lounge.
just like his flips and other tricks,
he won't let amy take his picture snoozing on the chaise lounge.
amy saw him and whispered to me;
"i'm going to get his picture this time."

so she got her camera and went to the window.
she lined up her shot,
and then i think he heard her finger touch the button
because he leapt to his feet
and stared accusingly at her in the window.
then he ran to his bigloo and went inside.

he was having such a nice nap in the sun...
until the paparazzi disturbed his peace again.
there is no privacy when you are a star.

the other morning i caught him unawares.

i was watching when he came out of the bigloo at first light.
he had heard sandra moving about,
but he doesn't pay her any attention.
she isn't going to run with him, or feed him, or pet him.
other than being one of the people under his charge,
she isn't that important in the start of his day.
her unexpectedly early noises must have disguised mine.

one of the big mysteries is how the hell he doesn't get his cable
wrapped around the trees.
he has 14 trees in reach of his cable,
but he never requires disentanglement.

we had to move sophie's cable
because there was one rock with a projection to catch it on.
she repeatedly got caught in the trap.
all she had to do was quit pulling to be free,
but we had to constantly go "rescue" her.

so that morning big came out of the bigloo.
he looked over to see sandra sitting at her computer.
he didn't see me hiding in the shadows.

six of his trees are in the area he has designated as his bathroom,
and in the adjacent space where he has his observation deck for
the woods behind the bigloo.
so big came out of his bigloo and stretched,
since no one significant was up yet,
he went back to attend to his business.

he went to the middle of the trees, and then off to one side to pee.
partway back and then over to his observation deck to check out
the woods.
then back to the middle of the trees again and over to another
spot to poop.

after another stint at the observation deck i was certain i'd be
going out to disentangle him.
watching him winding in and out around those trees,
there was no way he would be able to get out.

satisfied that all was well in the woods,
he turned and trotted back out thru the trees
and across his area to the place he waits for amy to open her
eyes.

his perfectly free cable trailed behind him.
he had never looked to see what was up with the cable.
somehow he was remembering which side of which tree he went
on, and when,
and then perfectly reversed it.

he lay down at the very end of his cable, butt to the back porch,
and stuck one hind leg out behind him.
then he put his head on his paws and waited for the sound of
amy's eyes opening...

i was watching him again when amy returned from her run with
sophie.
he was lying there, seemingly asleep, when amy must have
reached the place where the road passes nearest the bottom of
the hill.
she is still a half mile from home at that point,
but whenever we pass that spot we can hear big bark at us.

he suddenly jumped to his feet and started barking and wagging
his tail.
i knew where amy had to be.
then he was so happy that he took off running around his
perimeter.
he was winding thru the trees at breakneck speed,
and i could see the available cable rapidly diminishing.
as he came around the last tree, he had about 4 feet of cable left
and i braced myself to see him jerked off his feet.

he decelerated from a run to a walk,
took 2 more steps to reach the end of the cable
and stood there wagging his tail for a moment.
then he took off running back the way he had come.
exactly the way he had come,
unwinding himself until he was back where he had started.
he repeated the process a couple more times

by then he must have heard her coming up the driveway,
because he got real still and stood watching with total
concentration.

i could tell when she came in visual range,
because he started drumming his front feet...
right-left-right-left-right-left as fast as they would go.
as i heard the back door open he began barking furiously;
"hurry up! hurry up! it's time to go! HURRY UP!"

big would kill in a corn maze.

laz

## january 19, 2012
## ambassador big

during these days of no income i have become very conservative about driving.
errands that require going somewhere in a vehicle are consolidated until i leave the house at most once a week.
sometimes i go for several weeks without leaving.

big and little both share that canine love for "going for a ride"
we have always alternated, because there is no room for both in the car at once.
big overflows the front seat by himself.
little fits with room to spare, but not enough room for big.
nobody is allowed in the back seat,
because that is where the errand materials go...
trash for the dump, stuff to be mailed, etc, on the way out.
groceries or what not on the way home.

the good part of both dogs not fitting is we avoid the shotgun squabbles.
little and weiner used to tussle like 3 year olds,
both believing the prime shotgun spot belonged to them.

with trips so infrequent these days,
going for a ride is a bigger treat than ever
yesterday was big's day.
he was a lucky dog, because there were a lot of errands to run.

the first stop was the dump.
all the dogs love the dump trip.
it is like going to a doggie amusement park.
instead of rides, it has smells.
all sorts of wonderful aromas to tickle a dog's nose.
to begin with,
the whole ride over there are all those wonderful trash smells emanating from the back seat.
i used to take my truck, but these days it is all about gas conservation.

big always checks to see if (this time) i might allow him to go inspect the trash.
i always tell him he has to stay up front.
"there is your seat, big. that's where you belong."

likewise, at the dump he always checks to see if he can get out.
there are so many different odors that this has to be the most fascinating place on earth.

dump ritual behind, me and big went to check on the old house.
again, he had to wait in the car while i went inside.
i peeked out the window at him, and there was big inspecting the back seat.
after all there must be something really cool back there if he isn't allowed.

when i came out, there sat big in his seat, wearing his most innocent expression.
that is his "tell" that he has been up to something.
normally he (just like little) sits in my seat while he waits.
"you don't fool me, mr big. i know you've been in the back seat."
big just looked out the window.

the next stop was the bank.
it was a longer drive, and big tired of looking out the window.
he curled up on the front seat the best he could
(there is just more big than there is seat)
first he tried his head and shoulders hanging off in the floor.
that wasn't terribly comfortable.
"you try that every time, big. it never works. do you think you might get smaller, or that the seat will get bigger?"
big just grinned.

then he curled up with his butt wedged between the seat and the door and stretched his neck across the console so that his nose was touching me.
that is how we always end up,
altho if he has time to go to sleep his head will slip off the back of the console and he will sleep with it hanging between the seats into the back floorboard.

i thought about taking big into the bank.
there were no other customers there,
and he likes to make official visits in his role as pit bull
ambassador.
but there were still several stops to make,
so i left him sitting in my seat, waiting for me.

it's a funny thing about doing errands with big.
no matter where i stop,
if big waits in the car i can leave the car unlocked.
i can leave the keys in the ignition.
hell, i could leave the bank bag sitting on the dash.
big isn't one of those dogs that rages at passersby.
he just looks out at them calmly.
but no one seems inclined to try the door.

they always have a comment for me...
"i bet no one is going to break into that car!" is the usual one.
i guess not, since the only thing you can see is that bowling ball
size head,
two foot wide shoulders,
and a pair of big yellow eyes gazing at you.

as we were leaving the bank, another patron was arriving.
i could see him staring at big with a look of disgust as we were
backing out.
big just looked back at him out the passenger window.
poor big.

the next stop was the vet's office to pick up heartworm medicine.
i almost left big in the car
but a lady with a small dog was leaving as i got out.
big was looking out the windshield, off into space.
she commented; "oh, what a beautiful dog."
dont tell sandra, but big understands english.
he immediately came over to the window, wagging his tail for the
friendly lady.
i knew he would want to go inside.
he is an ambassador for big ugly dogs and there is nothing he
loves more than making friends.

i stuck my head in the office door before i let big come in.
i always have to be alert to the situations i introduce him to.
he isn't going to start trouble, but if someone had a poorly
restrained dog he couldn't go in.
trouble is always the fault of the pit.

in a recent newspaper article on a "vicious pit bull" in franklin
the report read:
"the police arrived to find the dog tied to a tree in the front yard."
then it added;
"while the police were there, it attacked a group of 3 other dogs."
the police were seeking to have the pit bull destroyed.

now, i was not there,
but how do you characterize a dog chained in its own yard being
attacked by a pack of 3 loose dogs as proof that the chained dog
is vicious?
call me crazy, but i think the owners of the loose dogs are the
ones at fault.

ambassador big has his work cut out for him.

the situation inside was ok, so we went in.
the young female receptionist has always been cool to big.
she likes dogs (she works at a vet's office!) but she has always
been aloof to big.
you can't blame her.
look at his potential and the reputation of his breed.

but big knows how to charm the ladies.
he just sort of positioned himself where he would be convenient
to pet.
he was, as always, careful not to stare,
but every time she looked in his direction he wagged his tail.
our business took a little time, as she was interupted by a couple
of calls.

finally, i could see her making a decision.
"you just want to be petted, don't you?"
big gave his most winning smile
(which i think makes him look rather like an amphibian)

and moved closer, tail wagging.
she reached down and petted his broad head.
big's expression was one of bliss.

a few moments later one of the assistants came out of the back.
this one has always liked big and she greeted him;
"well, hello big dog!"

big went over for some glorious full body petting.
a third girl came out, someone we hadn't seen before,
seeing the bigwich,
beaming with pleasure between the other two,
she just came over and joined in the fun.

of course, everyone had to get back to work so big's glorious
moment could only last a moment.
as everyone went about their business big started for the door to
the back.
i had a hard time convincing him to stay with me.
that was obviously the door leading to the ladies, and he wanted
to go find more.
big fancies himself quite the ladies man.

unfortunately they did not have the medicine in big's size.
so they sent me to another animal hospital just down the road.
emboldened by our success, i took big in again.
when i checked the inside there were no animals in the waiting
room at all.
only an older lady talking to the girl at the desk.

when me and big came in, the lady looked at big with horror and
disgust.
"those kind of dogs are vicious!"
"no, big is a sweetheart."
"they can't be trusted."
Big was securely on his leash and we went to the far end of the
counter.
none the less she kept a wary eye on big.

after a moment, big went as far as i let him in her direction,
and positioned himself to be petted.

she looked at him, big wagged his tail and looked away.
"mr big. not everyone wants to pet you."
big looked disappointed, but he came back and sat by me.

whatever she was doing was taking forever.
she would talk a while, then wait while the girl at the desk
bustled around, fussed with papers, or talked with someone on
the phone.

during one of the breaks she commented;
"he must have had intensive training to act like this. did you send
him to obedience school?"
"no, but i spend a lot of time with him. he is just a good natured
dog."

knowing he was the object of the conversation, big moved back
into petting postion.
the lady looked at him, but with more of an uncertain look.
"no, big, you shouldn't bother people who dont want to pet you."
big looked disappointed, but he came back and sat by me again.

a little later she had another wait,
and told me;
"i have heard that those dogs can just turn on you without
warning."
"people don't always pay attention to what is going on with their
dogs."

just then a woman dressed in scrubs came out of the back
heading for another door from the lobby.
she saw big and exclaimed;
"look at you, big fella. what a pretty boy!"

she crouched and i let big go to her for a hug and a moment of
serious petting.
"what is his name?"
"big"
"you named him right."
big just wagged his tail and buried his head in her lap.
his front end was engulfed, but his back end was wagging
happily.

the woman whispered where only i could hear;
"i have three of them at home. these are the best dogs there are."
"certainly the most intelligent."
i could not imagine three bigs. i would be the one living in a
bigloo.

after the woman went on about her business i could see the lady
looking at big thoughtfully.
big saw it too, and went back to his "available to pet" position.
a good ambassador knows how to handle delicate negotiations.

this time, i saw her tentatively hold out the back of her hand
towards big.
i let him sidle a little closer,
then he politely sniffed her hand and dropped his nose to leave
the top of his head in easy petting range.
she cautiously stroked the top of that massive head a few times
before pulling her hand back (intact!)
big came back and sat by me again.
this time he looked rather pleased with himself.

a few minutes later, the lady left.
i suspect that her story will be much the same as if she had
touched a live bear.
i doubt ambassador big has made an outright convert.
but there is probably one more person who knows big ugly dogs
are not all insane killers.

big was so wore out from the day that he skipped supper.
ambassador work is tougher than it looks.

laz

## january 23, 2012
## big talk

i was watching amy and big leave on patrol this morning...
always a funny sight,
big with that huge grin and his eyes bugging out with excitement.
tiny amy trailing behind, like a pixie on a string.

you can count on big being in a hurry to get out on the course.
amy just finished running with sophie, and i can almost read
big's thoughts;
"god, i can't believe amy took that skinny headed dog out on my
road. who knows what kind of mess she has left out there."

as they reached the back porch i saw amy tell big to stop.
then she leaned over and said something in his ear.
big listened thoughtfully,
then he started back out at a much more reserved pace.

i knew what amy had told him.
she had said;
"if you want a run this morning, you are going to have to stop
pulling."

amy commented to me the other day that;
"you know, i talk to big just like he is a person.
i never baby talk big like i do with sophie and little.
it kind of seems like he would be offended."

i do the same thing.
it drives sandra crazy, but i talk to big just like he was a person.
i answered amy;
"yeah. i would stop if it didn't seem like he understood
everything i said."

i would not testify in court that dog understands english.
i know better.
but i wouldn't talk around him about anything i didn't want him
to know.
i act like he understands, without even thinking about it.

like the day i told him out of the blue;
"do you want a treat? do a flip and i'll give you a treat."
big jumped high in the air and spun a 360.
technically it wasn't a flip, but he has to be at the end of his cable
to do a proper flip.
i gave him the treat.

the other day i got careless and let him step over the slack in his
leash.
when this happens to little or sophie you have to hold them still
and pick their foot up to disentangle them
(while they jump around in excitement)
attempts to get them to step back over the leash end up with
them running in circles and winding theirself up even worse.

with big i said;
"stop"
then i flipped the leash against the back of his leg and said;
"pick up your foot so i can get the leash out."
he picked that foot up while i pulled the leash under it, and we
continued on our way.

and that is how we operate.
"let's cross the road, big."
and we walk across.
"no big, we are going the other way."
and he goes the other way.
"wait over there."
and he goes over there to wait.

some of our deals are pretty complex.
back when i started bringing him up on the porch to play on
rainy days i told him;
"do you want off your leash? i'll let you off your leash, but you
have to stay on the porch."
and that is just what he has done.

once in a while he'll see a squirrel or a bird, and go over to the
steps and look. i can see he is wanting to go, but i tell him;
"don't even think about it, big. you have to stay up here."
he will turn around and come back...

98

until the other day.
it wasn't raining at the moment, but we were between storms.
we were on the porch playing "can that dog jump?" and other big games.
big was having a ball
and then he stopped and looked at me with a twinkle in his eye that i didn't quite trust.
"what are you thinking, mr big?"

the words hardly escaped my mouth when big turned and raced down the steps and over to the dogpen.
"BIG! you better come back up here RIGHT NOW!"
big acted like he didn't know i was there.
as i started down the steps, big raced past me and out to the start of the driveway.
"BIG! COME ON BIG!"

big was making a big show of sniffing at a tree until i got close, and then he shot down the driveway to the trail crossing and began looking both ways as if making up his mind which way to go.
"BIG! I DO NOT WANT TO PLAY 'CATCH ME IF YOU CAN!' I DO NOT LIKE THAT GAME!"

i gave him one more chance.
but when he dashed on down the driveway to the little house i followed him gathering good throwing rocks as i went.
down at the little house, i found big fascinated by something in the flowerbeds.

"catch me if you can" seems to require that he be absorbed by something until you get almost within reach.
this time the game changed.
as he took off i zinged a rock at him.
i missed, and the rock bounced underneath his belly and across the road.
big stopped dead.

he looked where the rock had gone,
and then he looked back at me.
i already had my arm cocked to throw again,

99

but the rock hit empty space.
big can go from zero to sixty in 0.01 seconds.
he circled wide around me and was out of range up the driveway
before i could get the next rock ready.
(i think he has a 40 time in the low 2's)

he was out of sight when i got to where the driveway curves into
the woods.
as i walked back up the driveway i was muttering all sorts of dire
threats to myself.
i looked both ways down the trail, lest he had taken a side track,
but there was no sign of big anywhere.
"you better be on the porch or in the bigloo, if you know what's
good for you."

when i finally reached the porch, i didn't see him at first.
then he came out of his hiding place behind the fireplace, his face
a picture of contrition.
his tail wagging, head low, begging for forgiveness.

i punished him severely.
i spoke harshly to him and didn't pet him.
ok, i didn't pet him until we got to the bigloo.
"if you do that again, big, we won't be able to play on the porch
anymore."

there have been no repeat offenses.
but that is just a coincidence, right?
we all know that dogs can't understand english.

laz

## january 31, 2012
## big's 3-churches run

me and big had been talking about it since we first did our
millersburg church route.
we could go out millersburg road to millersburg church
and instead of coming back, take hoovers gap-christiana road
(passing community of christ church in plainview at the midway
point)
then back to short creek church on short creek road
and then home.

we were figuring it would take about 3 hours.
most days we only get 2 hours, and then me and little do 2 more.
yesterday i planned to spend the afternoon doing repairs on the
driveway, digging out the potholes and paving them with stone.
little loves to help with chores and would be plenty happy to
forego her walk to provide little assistance with my driveway
repairs.

it was chilly when we started
but i was somewhat underdressed because we knew it would
warm up as the day went on.
big's breath came out in huge puffs of steam
my feet crunched on the gravel, the potholes i would be filling in
the afternoon were crusted over with ice.
the long walk thru the woods is always so filled with
anticipation,
you never know what is waiting once we get out on the road.

as we crest the little rise in front of the winston place we enter a
postcard. the distant line of the highland rim hills in the distance,
the sun just rising into the sky above them
mr winston's pastures running up to the wooded hills on the
right, his scattered cows grazing peacefully
ben's hayfields running off to the distant woods on the left
our little valley as quiet as an empty church.
i can see 4 deer moving along the edge of the woods in mr
winston's pasture,
preparing to head up into the hills for the day.

big is doing his own morning sightseeing,
snuffling his nose back and forth on the road,
reading the scent messages.
he knows about every animal that has crossed the road during
the night.

we pass alongside sections of ancient, moss covered stone walls.
i never tire of the intricate patterns of the stone,
and i often imagine what it looked like a century ago,
when they were new and clean and gleaming white freshly
mined limestone...
enclosing the farms of different generations of bens and
winstons.

i see a hawk gliding thru the air, about 20 feet above the hayfield
searching the ground for voles or rabbits.
i wonder if it is one of the pair that raised their young in the big
hackberry tree last summer,
or a new hawk searching for its own territory.
it passes within 50 feet of me and big and i marvel at the
wingspan.
i think it is a larger bird that the one we watched all last summer.

i do not spot mr winston's little donkey herd.
after we watched the mating chases at the end of last summer,
thru the fall and early winter they had been split into two groups,
with the three jacks traveling together,
talking, no doubt, about burro sports and jennys in heat.
the jennys and last year's foals had stuck together in their own
little herd.
talking, no doubt, about the playful yearlings,
the growing bellies of the mothers to be,
and which is the hottest jack.
one day soon both groups will disappear into the wooded hills
for about a month. when they return they will be traveling with a
couple of big eyed foals and the jacks will stand guard over the
herd, eyeing big with suspicion as we pass.

i found their foaling grounds last year, high up in the wooded
rocky hills,
safe from spying eyes of predators.

we cross over creeks, rushing with waters as the ample recent
rains are draining from the hills and the fields.

we come to ben's winter wheat fields,
and they are bright green carpets.
when they were planted in december,
the sprouts came up rapidly
until the fields appeared to be covered by a pale green mist.
then the sprouts paused.

for most of december and january all the activity was
underground
as the billions of tiny plants put down root systems to support
the growth to come.
in the past few days, their emphasis has shifted and the pale
green mist is gone
replaced by a lush green carpet of rapidly growing wheat stalks.

as we get further into spring there will be another shift
as the plants stop growing and focus on storing up the energy to
put into a final push of the growth cycle...
the production of grain.
for it is the grain that gives them their dominance over man,
inducing man to tend their young for another generation.
(what? are you under the misapprehension that man has tamed
plants, rather than the other way around?)

the rhythms of the seasons, the plants, and the animals
are as old as the rhythms of the generations who keep these
farms in our little hidden valley.
as big and i stride down the road, i feel like a part of the timeless
scenes around me.

then we leave the valley and enter the woods.
it is the mighty tree trunks of the oldest trees that catch my eye.
last summer the hickory trees did not produce,
and it has been a difficult winter for the squirrels
(and probably deer as well)
the oaks did alright,
but a total absence of hickory nuts in these hickory dominated
forests means hard times for many.

i wonder how the trees all manage to plan together
the years of plenty, and the years of famine.
last year, the hickory nuts fell on our roof like rain.
this year, i have not seen a single nut.


before i know it,
we are passing thru the scattered houses of millersburg.
we turn at the church, and a few hundred yards more carries us
to the creek bordered by an old rock wall,
where we have always turned around.
past here is all new territory.


as we walk on we pass thru large beautiful farms with manicured
pastures.
amazing rockwork, that you would never notice from a car,
much of it is so beautiful that we cross the road to take a better
look.
some are fences made from the rock picked from the fields to
make it suitable for farming.
they speak of countless hours of work.
hard, manual labor by the ancestors of todays farmers and
burros.
others are made from quarry stone.
they speak of wealthy farmers from a time gone by.


as we pass one pasture a small herd of horses runs up to the
fence, eyeing me and big with great interest.
one young stallion seems to want to play with big.
tossing his head and snorting at big,
before dashing off a short ways and then returning to try again.
big struggles with the temptation to join in the chase.


i won't let him go,
so he sends one of his pee mails,
and then throws up a roostertail of dirt
before looking to see just what his prospective playmate thinks.
"i don't think horses are impressed by pee mails, mr big."
he seems doubtful of my words.


we pass the line of the giant metal power poles that carry some
main electrical stream.

104

looking back down their cleared path, until it gets small,
we can just see where the line crosses over the hills on the
Winston's place.
"we were there only an hour ago, big guy."
big is, as usual, much more interested in what is immediately
around us.

on we go.

as we approach the community of christ church, there is another
small scattering of houses.
we are in plainview.
hidden in the woods, we see an ancient rock walled yard around
the crumbling ruins of an old house.
another landmark of a time gone by that is invisible to people
rushing past in cars.

the walk goes on and on.
we pass fantastic hundred year old houses, and hidden ponds.
woods and hills.

i start to tell big that we are probably getting close to short creek
road, and there it is right in front of us.
the time has flown by.

we pass by one house, and there is an odd "peeping" sound
coming from the yard.
as we come around the house i see a large dog in a pen.
he is making all the motions of barking at us, but only emitting a
tiny peeping sound.
the unfortunate animal has been debarked.

later on, another small dog is in a front yard on a chain.
except he has only about 4 feet of play.
most of the chain is tangled into a soccer ball sized knot.
what would a cable cost, 15 or 20 dollars?

the thoughtless cruelties we casually heap on "man's best friend"
are staggering.

we pass a spotless farm, comandeered by a shanty put together
from scraps of wood and metal.
the yard appears to be scoured clean.
a weathered mailbox is nailed to a post at the road.
in place of a name or address it is covered with little stick on
letters saying;
"keep out", "no trespassing", and "violaters will be persecuted."
i assume the owner is not the community social director.

much of his farm has been grazed by too many goats for too
many years.
barren, rocky, and devoid of soil it sports only scrubby cedars,
and a few weeds.
it won't even support goats now.

we see a cat crossing the road in front of us.
big is indignant.
i will never understand his hatred of "nasty cats."
i won't let him pursue it, so he settles for leaving a pee mail
and kicking up another rooster tail.
"bigness, i don't think cats give a darn about pee mails."
he looks at me doubtfully.

finally we come to the goat corner farm,
and we are back on our familiar route.

i could tell you more about the rest of our walk,
but i have probably bored you to death by now.
we made the distance in 2:50.

by the end of the afternoon,
chopping out the potholes all the way to the underlying soil,
and then paving the hole with fitted stones
(some weighing in the hundreds of pounds)
i was thoroughly pooped.

it was a wonderful day on the farm.
and me and big are already making plans to do the lynch hill
loop. i can only imagine the wonders we will see there.

laz

## february 04, 2012
## another pit-human encounter

despite the relative impossibility of keeping big contained at all
times, he has done a pretty good job of establishing himself as a
neighborhood fixture.

he was not welcomed on his arrival in short creek.
i threw rocks at him.
someone else shot him.
but his steady good nature seems to have won everyone over.

this morning was another race with the rain.
amy and big had to wait on one round to finish before going out.
and i checked the radar when they got back,
calculating that we *probably* could get in 3 more miles before the
next round came thru.

and i would have been right, if big didn't have so many friends.

we got halfway around the dead coyote 3-mile course before we
saw dale pulling out of his driveway.
dale is on the big walking team,
so he stopped and rolled down his window;
"hello big!"

big wanted to jump up and look in the window,
but dale's car is too nice,
so i told him not to jump on the car.
big sat down to wait while we talked about the dead coyote.
i figure by summer i ought to be able to collect his skull.
then dale told big goodbye and went on his way.

when we got started back
i could see the dark clouds were really close.
"i think we can still make it big. but we can't fool around."

as we approached the miller place,
i saw mr miller coming out to get his mail.

big didn't see him at first,
he was busy ignoring the miller's little dog.
they call it a miniature doberman.
it is chihuahua sized,
but the exact black and tan colors as a doberman
and the same basic build.
it even has the cropped ears and tail.

he always has fits when he sees me and big coming by.
he barks and bristles and raises cain...
and doesn't come into the road until we have passed.
his bark sounds like a munchkin bark.
(i think he huffs helium when he sees us coming)
it probably doesn't help his self image when me and big laugh at
him.

anyway, big and mr miller spotted each other at about the same
time. mr miller waved and big started wagging his tail and
pulling with all his might.
mr miller pets big, and big doesn't want to miss a petting.
we got there quickly.

while mr miller petted big he commented;
"i can't believe the rain isn't here yet."
"yeah, we checked the radar before we left. i think we can make
it back, but its gonna be close."

the millers have another dog.
it is really old, and seldom comes out unless one of the millers is
already outside.
it is barely bigger than the chihuahua dog.

about this time it realized that its master was petting big.
with a ferocious snarl, it charged big,
jumped up,
and bit him on the lip.

big jumped back and looked at him with amazement.
apparently realizing the foolishness of his action,
the little dog retreated into its yard and settled for threatening
barks and growls.

108

mr miller gave big another pat,
while looking up at the sky,
and said;
"i better let y'all go if you're going to beat the rain."

we were doing good.
and then, only about a half mile from the house,
we saw ben in his truck.
ben stopped and rolled down his window;
"hello big!"

i am starting to wonder who is walking who,
and when did i become big's wingman?
i told ben enthusiatically about the new 3-churches course.
then we talked about the lynch hill course.

ben hasn't run it yet either,
and i warned him if he didnt hurry,
me and big would beat him to it.
"we've been talking about it since we knocked off the 3-churches
run."
ben laughed.

we always tell him he is the undisputed top runner in the entire
greater short creek area.
then he said;
"i better let you go if you're going to get home before the rain."

as ben's tailgate went by the first few drops started to splat on
the pavement around us.
"i think we are going to get caught, big. you have too many
friends."
it progressed from isolated drops to a downpour in about 10
steps. big does not like the rain, and was pulling like mad.
i don't care for it myself, and was happy to have big pull me
rapidly down the road.

when we reached the end of the driveway i told big to "stop."
he didn't really want to, but orders are orders.
then i unhooked his leash and asked him if he wanted to go wait
on the porch.

it didn't really register and he took a few more steps in formation
before realizing his leash was not attached.
big stopped and looked back at me.

i told him;
"go on and get out of the rain, big guy. wait for me on the porch
and i'll be right behind you."
i didn't have to tell him again.
the next thing i saw was his big red behind disappearing around
the corner into the woods.

a few minutes later, when i got to the house,
amy was out on the porch toweling big off.
she told me she had looked out the window;
"and there was big, standing on the edge of the porch looking
back down the driveway."

big gave me a look that said;
"i thought you were going to be 'right behind me?'"
"hey, i came as fast as i can. i only have 1 good leg, you got 3."

big, amy, and myself spent a pleasant rest of the morning on the
porch, watching it rain and talking.
amy will be going to massachusetts before too long.
me and big are gonna miss her.

laz

## february 06, 2012
## big errors

well, he finally did it.
i had been feeling a little foolish
because i always worry about big being out on his cable when
there is no one around for a long time.
i'd hate for him to get trapped out in the weather.
but he simply never got tangled.

i was watching him play the other day.
he was tossing his bone in the air,
and chasing it down and pouncing on it then tossing it up again.
he finally got so excited that he started running in a circle around
the central tree where his cable is attached.
around and around he went, butt tucked under, and flying.
naturally the available cable got shorter and shorter until he was
almost to the tree.

then he turned and rocketed back the other way,
unwinding his cable round after round,
and making his circle bigger and bigger.

he stopped one round shy of being completely unwound, and i
thought;
"hah, mr big. you miscounted."
he trotted over to his water bowl to get a drink and came up a
little short of where he normally can reach.
he stopped and looked thoughtful for just a moment.
then he turned and reared up on his hind legs like a horse,
before launching himself and racing back around the tree one
more time.

it wasn't until the next day that he proved himself only human.
i came out on the back porch and saw big standing among the
little cluster of trees at the back of his area.
normally he will come running over to the near side of his area,
hoping for a visit.
it always amazes me to see him weave thru the trees and emerge
with his cable unfettered.

this time he just stood there looking at me.
"is something wrong, big fella?"
big gave a short "help me" bark and continued to look at me.

i went back to find that big had gotten himself into a mess.
he had gone around one tree on the west side.
then another tree on the west side.
followed by circling around on the east side
and cutting back west between them and going under the
crossing cable,
then coming back to the east side and going over the crossing
cable, creating a knot..
he had obviously recognized the importance of going over and
under...

but he got the sequence wrong.
he had gone back under and returned going over again.
instead of untying his knot, he had tied a second knot.
this is where he proved just how close to human he really is.
having tried to solve a problem by a method that he believed in,
and it not working,
the obvious solution was to do it again.
and again and again and again and...

he had tied a neat row of six knots before he ran out of cable.
(my god, he could run for office)

i had to unhook him while i untied it.
big was grateful, he'd never had any doubt that i could fix it.

but big isn't the only one making errors.
he is always trying to warn amy of the mistake that it is to take
sophie when she runs.

he doesn't think sophie is very brave.
maybe because sophie will run to his area,
then when he comes to play she rolls over on her back.
she did that again just the other day.
i saw amy on the porch with sophie, scrubbing her down.
"sophe is all covered in mud" she told me.

"big was pushing her around his area with his nose, trying to get
her to get up and play."
"i don't know why she still goes there?"

sophie cant seem to get it thru her head that she really
(really, really, really)
 doesn't want to play with big.

amy and i were on the porch with big.
sophie and little were at the door looking out.
they wanted to come out and play.
it was amy's turn for an error.

she opened the door without looking.
little shot out, with sophie on her heels (they are the dog team)
little and big met in midair,
with all the sounds of a full-scale dog war.

sophie, recognizing her error too late, dropped and rolled.
big thought it was the ultimate game; two on one!
he knocked little back with his chest and whipped around to grab
sophie by the throat.
sophie let out a loud yelp of terror
(it was too hectic to notice, but odds are she peed herself)

big, startled, let go and jumped back
his expression reminded me of when i was a teenager and boys
and girls would play tackle football together.
you would grab a girl to tackle her, and she would squeal.
you immediately let go, not sure what it was you might have
grabbed.
(of course, the girl would then take off running again)

big didn't have time to worry about sophie,
little jumped him from behind and they went back at it.
sophie was only too glad to let amy lead her back in the house.

we broke big and little up after a couple more minutes.
their game is not really an appropriate porch game,
and i didn't want to do the dog-cleaning job that follows big and
little games in the mud.

right now i am watching big reclining on his lounge chair.
he is looking at sophie and little like they are idiots.
they are in the pen
(the one that contained big for a day has held them for 2 years)
barking and barking at some imaginary something.
i have learned to pay no attention to them either.

when big barks, someone is coming or something is going on.
if big don't bark, there ain't nothin' to see.
sophie & little bark because they are...

the short bus dogs.

big can act pretty smug,
but i know the truth now. he isn't perfect.
big makes errors, too.
he is only human after all.

laz

**february 11, 2012**
**the big cold wave**

winter almost didn't come this year.
altho we've had enough rain for 10 winters,
the temperatures have been fabulous.
60's during the day, 40's at night.
it has been the best "winter" ever.

today winter paid us a visit.
temperatures in the teens and spitting snow,
howling winds to drive the cold thru your clothes and right down
to the skin.
if i didn't have a big, this would be a perfect rest day.
big doesn't believe in rest days.

i looked out the window, and sure enough there sat big.
as close to the back porch as he could get, one leg stuck out,
just to be that much closer.
there was snow drifting on his back.

ok. i owe it to him.
so i bundled up the best i could.
thank god for the coat that got abandoned after the backyard
ultra.
it has a hood!

i put on my little cotton gloves, and knew they would be
inadequate. i searched all over the house for a stray pair of
leather work gloves. leather gloves over those little jersey gloves
is really pretty warm.
i knew i wouldn't find any, but i had to try.

unfortunately i have already worn out my last pair of leather
gloves.
(doing that "work" stuff, that i think makes me more valuable
than a keurig)
financial hard times has a higher price than just having an empty
belly a lot of the time.
my hands were going to get cold.

big was elated to see me.
he jumped around with excitement
and shook all the snow off his back.
once we were on our way it was hard to get him calmed down to
stop pulling.
amy didn't run with him this morning (cold-wimp!)
and he always pulls more when he hasn't had a run first to take
some of the edge off.

the wind was rifling through my clothes like a pickpocket,
trying to find a way in,
so it could run its frigid fingers over my flesh.
but i was pretty thoroughly bundled and frustrated its icy
ambitions.

my body core was plenty warm.
my insulated boots were doing a good job for my feet.
only my hands uncomfortable.
i would have loved to stick them down in my pockets,
but one had to hold the leash,
and the other had to hold the dog trainer.

we would walk a while, as snow piled up on big's back
then i would say "STOP"
and big would stand still so i could brush it off.
the other time we walked in the snow it was just above freezing
and the snow melted as soon as it landed on him,
getting him thoroughly wet.

i didn't want to bring him home wet in this weather.
the high quality of his fur coat was evident,
as the snow remained frozen despite being within a half inch of
his warm body.
i still didn't want to chance getting him wet,
so i kept knocking it off.

i explained to big that it wasn't going to be a long walk today.
and we were going to try to stick to the more sheltered roads.
he didn't really care about anything except that we were walking
now...
and he had pee mails to post on the dog list.

lynnor's nasty little pug didn't make a peep today.
as a matter of fact none of the usual dogs barked at us.
they lacked big's dedication to the schedule.

none the less, big stopped after we passed their houses,
to leave a pee mail and kick up a rooster tail of dirty snow.
after a couple of tries he cut back on kicking up dirt.
the frozen ground was like scratching on concrete.

at one point i thought i heard a train.
when the weather is right we can sometimes hear trains passing
thru fosterville.
except the sound was coming from the wrong direction.
i looked up on the hillside and could see trees whipping around
as a wall of wind came down the hill towards us.
"this stinks, big. don't you know this stinks?"
big looked up at me and grinned.

i bet he was thinking;
"no, you fool. 100 degrees stinks. this is great!"
the only reason i wasn't worried about my fingers getting
frostbite was that they hurt.
i figured i was safe as long as they didn't get numb.
"no, mr big. trust me, this stinks."

as we approached the place i had chosen to turn around
we saw the pyrrhenies that guards the goats on the bell farm.
usually he watches us from the field,
but today he had come down and was standing in the road.
as we got closer i could see that he was barking at us.
i could'nt hear it, because the wind was blowing his barks away.
it was like watching a silent movie of a dog barking.

today big decided he wasn't in walking past and ignoring mode.
he started pulling and wanting to get fiesty as we got near the
pyrrhenies.

it couldn't have come on a better day.
we wouldn't lose much of our walk at all demonstrating to big
who was in charge.

i told him;
"ok big. if that's how it is we'll just go home."
i turned around and the big immediately transformed into his
best behavior.

big might have been dismayed
(and no doubt resolving not to break protocol again)
but i just felt great relief.
we had walked into the wind all the way out,
and now it was at our back.
it was as if the temperature had risen 20 degrees.

the walk home was actually pleasant.

as we neared the house, the weekend mail-lady drove past us.
we see her often, but usually way out on our fosterville route.
we were getting home a lot earlier than usual today.
since ben's house is the last one on the mail route
i knew she would be back by with our mail in a few minutes.
so me and big waited for her by the mailbox.

when she stopped she peered out at us thru the window.
"that is a scary looking dog."
"he is a sweetheart."
"that's what everyone says. but it is their dog. that is a scary
looking dog. i bet he can smell my fear."

indeed, big must have known she was afraid.
he had stood up to look in the window when she arrived,
but he didn't go up to make himself available to pet.
"move back a little, big. you are scaring the mailman."
big backed away, and she handed me the mail.

we went on up to the house for breakfast.
the morning petting session wasn't as long as usual,
because i was *cold*, even though the porch is mostly sheltered
from the north wind.

when we got to the big house, he was still feeling his wheaties,
so we took some time to play some of his favorite games.

we played "flip your bone in the air and race in circles"
we played "run back and forth past laz, and jump as high as his
head every time past"
we even played "run into your bigloo at 100 miles an hour and
do a 180 without slowing down."

of course big does the running and jumping.
my job is to cheer and encourage him.
i forgot how cold it was,
laughing at the big and his stunts.
eyes wide, mouth open, tongue flapping in the breeze,
he would tear around like a crazy dog for a minute
creating a tremendous uproar.
then suddenly stop perfectly still
and the only sound would be the panting of his breath.

just as suddenly he would take back off.
every minute of big games is probably as much exercise as a mile
of walking.
it finally wore him down.
he stopped and came over to stand against my leg and get petted
for just a moment.

then he grinned up at me,
went over and got his bone
and settled down to chew.

i think he had just told me to;
"go on in and get out of the cold."

what can i say. we humans are soft.
i did what he suggested.

laz

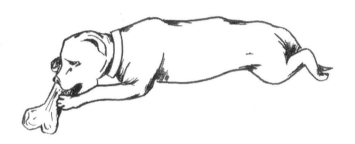

**february 15, 2012**
**big speed**

we havent played "catch me if you can" since the day i chucked a
rock at the big.
who'd have ever thought it was that easy?

with big converted to the school of "come when called"
i have been working in opportunities for him to do stuff without
a leash.
big likes that a lot,
because it allows him to go at his natural speed.
big just has two factory installed settings:
off, and big speed.

he is in the off setting right now,
reclining in the sun on his chaise lounge.
of course he got on the chaise lounge at full out big speed.

i was a little early this morning when i came out with his big blue
leash, big was in the midst of doing some sort of business in his
area. his cable was wound among the trees.

when he saw me coming around the corner, big forgot all about
the necessity of retracing his route thru the trees.
big took off at big speed, straight for me,
abruptly stopping about 10 feet later when his cable pulled taut
against a small tree.
as we all know, big is only human.

and what happens to us humans when we try to hurry?
we end up taking twice as long.
rather than stopping to figure out which way to unwind,
big took off in the same direction, making a huge circle around
the tree.
when he wasn't unwound, he simply picked up speed.
(even the worst plan will work, if you just try harder, right?)
as i came across the yard,
big was racing in an ever diminishing circle.

the cable was wrapping around and around and around the tree,
turning it into a gray barber shop pole.
by the time i got to him big had stopped with about two feet of
cable left.
"you have to unwind yourself mr big."
he started to go forward again.
"no big fella, you're going the wrong way."

big stopped and looked up at me.
i grabbed the tree with one hand, and started around in the
proper direction.
big caught on and raced back around the tree, with me hopping
the cable as he passed.
when i caught him, he did it again, me hopping the cable as he
passed.
after a few rounds, i could keep up with the cable while big ran
full speed in a rapidly growing circle.
i ran around the tree as fast as i could go, head down watching
the cable.
as big finished the last round and was loose,
i let go of the tree and started over to join him...

have you ever seen a dizzy bat contest?

leaning at about a 45 degree angle,
i stumbled sideways, very nearly going down.
i stopped with my hands on my knees while i waited on my head
to quit spinning.
"you're gonna have to give me a minute, big. have you ever seen
a dizzy bat contest?"
while he waited, big remembered his business, finished
unwinding himself from the trees and got a drink.
by then i was ready to go.

after that he had finished his morning 5 miler, had breakfast, and
spent some cuddle time on the porch.
as always, with his nap on schedule next, big's eyelids were
getting pretty heavy.
he was glad when i gave the word.
"ok, mr big. you about ready for your morning nap?"
big hopped up and ran out to the pedestal beside the steps.

122

when i go down the steps he is at head height there,
perfect for a big hug.
the big hug is an integral part of heading out to the big
homestead.

after his big hug, i tell him "alright, lets go"
and the big leaps high into the air and hits the landing at a run.
he races to little and sophie's pen, where he sniffs about.
when i catch up, he races on.

this morning it was nice and sunny,
so i was bringing his chaise lounge.
big raced to where we set up his lounge chair in the morning,
at 90 miles an hour.
as usual he overshot his mark by about 20 feet.
big never calculates in decelleration.
"you jumped the gun, big. we gotta hook up your cable first."

big tilted his head at me a moment,
and then took off for the bigloo.
(that is where we left the end of the cable this morning)
he shot past the door of the bigloo and out into the woods, trying
to decellerate.
all the while i am walking toward the bigloo at laz speed.
(my own natural settings are: off, slow, really slow, and glacial)

big had time to mark a tree outside his normal range
and then came rocketing back as i approached the bigloo.
he shot past between me and the door of the bigloo,
ending up all the way back where his lounge chair would go.
big looked at me panting.
i leaned his lounge chair against the bigloo
(never set it on the ground until you are ready for it to contain a
big)
and picked up his cable.

"lets get it done, big guy."
this time big came straight at me.
it was like standing in a bobsled run,
with a hairy, grinning bobsled coming downhill.
i have learned to have my legs spread apart,

but big's wide body still brushes against both sides as he passes
thru. it is lucky for both of us that i am a little bowlegged.
he executes his 180 and a massive head pops out between my
knees grinning up at me.

i clip on his cable and then with practiced precision hop over his
cable as big shoots back off for his lounging spot.
when i get there and set down his lounge chair big gets on it the
inimitable big way.
he leaps high in the air and comes down in the center with all 4
feet.
his chair bounces under the impact and then big is down,
ready to nap in the sun.
big's possessions just don't have a long life expectancy.

this afternoon we will reverse the process to come up on the
porch for supper.
except with a more demanding ritual.
as i unhook big i will tell him;
"now you have to walk with me big. you can't run ahead."

after i unhook him he will take 2 running steps then stop
abruptly and look back at me.
when i get beside him he will take two running steps, stop
abruptly, and look back at me.
and that's how we cross the yard.
me walking at a normal pace, big jerking across the yard in high
speed stops and starts...

until i relent and tell him;
"ok"
then he is off like a shot,
his stocky body skidding into a right angle turn at the steps
and flying up to the back door, to look in and see if amy is there.
if amy is home, she might come out and pet him.
then he hurries over to the table where his food bowl is sitting
and stands up on his hind legs to see what he has.
"same thing as the last 150 days, big. sorry."
when i was "rich" (ie employed) sometimes we had meat,
and big might have a little bit of fat,
or a drizzle of grease on top of his food.

124

i'm not sure why he looks, because with that nose of his,
he always knows when there is a treat as soon as i step out the
door.

the return trip is just like the morning trip,
with his mandatory stop halfway to check out the pen,
except he will race, hell for leather, straight to the bigloo
and shoot in the front door, the impact bouncing it across the
ground.
with a loud bumping and thumping he executes a full-speed 180
and out pops his big head to await the cable.
big's possessions just dont have a long life expectancy,
altho the super bigloo has survived much better than the first
model.

when i get there i have to tell him;
"you gotta come out for a minute mr big, so i can scoot your
bigloo back where it belongs."
he will come out while i return it to its proper place,
then he gets back in and sticks his head out again.
i give him a last pet on the head and tell him;
"you get a good sleep big guy and i will see you in the morning."
big just grins at me. it has been another perfect day...
lived at big speed.

laz

**february 18, 2012**
**the big half marathon**

big set a pr today.
in a small impromptu race that no one ever heard of...

until now.

big and i had been planning to do the lynch hill loop at the first
opportunity.
today looked like it. plenty of time and good weather in the
forecast.
i had a good course measurement (a little over 12 miles)
and we had scouted out much of the course for possible dog
issues.
the most dangerous section seemed likely to be when we passed
thru the main part of millersburg (7 houses)
so we had already done that during our 6 miler thursday.
there were a couple of dog issues, but we had things worked out
pretty well.

at last night's ball game, i asked dale if he wanted to go with us.
he did; so the lynch hill half marathon was on!

in light of last week's prophetic thread about dogs
(which many seemed to find somehow unrelated to
ultrarunning)
the final outcome of the day seemed eerily predestined.

the course itself was gorgeous.
a combination of woods and farms,
fantastic scenery, some impressive overlooks
and of course a couple of tough climbs
(without which overlooks are not possible)

but the story today turned out to be dogs.
altho dale and/or me and big had been over most of the course,
knew where the dogs were, and how to handle each one,
we had not been over it all.
and in one of the new places i had one of those rare events:

a truly serious dog encounter.
for those of you who live in places with leash laws,
here is how it is when you run in tennessee.

we come to the first dogs, the trailer dogs, about a mile out.
the black dog must have finally bitten someone,
because he has been chained for a couple of weeks now.
this makes passing the trailer a whole lot easier.
the white dog comes to the edge of the road,
snarling and baring its teeth.
it acts real threatening,
but having already encoutered the trainer,
and having been whacked with ben's stick,
it doesn't come into the road after pedestrians anymore.

we dont come to another dog for two glorious miles
until we have to go thru greater metropolitan millersburg.
first there are a border collie and a small brown dog of unknown
lineage (if it is a breed, it is a breed i am unfamiliar with)
the first time we went thru, they acted like they might be trouble,
but they respect big's size and merely bark from the yard now.
then we come to the trailer trash beagles.
i expected trouble when i saw the junkyard/home the first time.
mean dogs must be trailer trash viagra.

one of them always peels off early.
the other one would be a problem if i didn't have big.
when ben runs this way, he will almost certainly have to whack it
with his stick.
it is a nuisance for about a quarter mile,
trying to sneak in behind us,
but threats are enough to keep it away.

the trailer trash beagle passes us off to a huge yellow dog.
this dog barks, runs at us, and acts bad.
but it won't come into the road until we are past.

3 miles in, 4 loose dog encounters.
none were serious today,
altho the trailer trash beagle will eventually require an up close
and personal with the trainer.

128

unquestionably he will be a nuisance as long as he lives,
and when he dies they will get another nuisance dog and it will
start all over.


dale is amazed at big's ability to just continue walking
and not respond to dogs barking and running at him.
later on he will get to see just how accomplished big is.


the next mile and a half are new territory.
there aren't many houses,
and we are lucky enough that if there are loose dogs,
we dont see them.
at 4.5 miles we reach the furthest dale has come from the other
direction.
there is a dog here that he is afraid to pass.
part of our purpose is to show dale how to deal with dogs.
all of his routes are limited by dogs that turn him back.


none the less, we are all just as happy when that dog doesn't
make an appearance today.


the next 2 miles have no inhabited houses
and we can walk with impunity and enjoy the day.


at 7 miles, this changes and we pass a series of houses with loose
dogs. the first is a fat black dog that usually harrasses dale.
it takes one look at big and runs up on the porch to bark at us.


then there is a little lap-warmer outside a trailer
it usually barks at dale from the side of the road.
it takes one look at big and runs to hide under the trailer.


dale thinks big is pretty useful.


but the next dog is another big yaller dog.
it usually doesn't bother dale,
but today its masters are outside.
so it comes running out barking at us.
i tell dale that i find dogs to be worse when their master is
around.
they are braver and still not under control.

i point the trainer at it, and the point is taken.
the dog stops and continues barking,
but doesn't come out in the road until we are past.

then we pass a couple of pyrrhenies in a pasture with livestock.
there is a big sign on the fence that says:

GUARD DOGS ON DUTY.
PLEASE RESTRAIN ALL PETS
TO AVOID INCIDENTS

they come to the fence and watch us walk past.
these dogs know their job and do it.
they prove that dogs just dont have to be an issue...

if people only knew their job and did it.

one dog to go.

it is a monstrous husky with which dale has a tentative
understanding.
it has always let him pass,
but not without menacing him.
it seems to have different ideas about big.
it is on the side of the road kicking up grass and looking bad,
as we get closer it comes out in the middle of the road and faces
us, bristling.

i tell dale to pick up some rocks,
as there is a pile conveniently close to the road.
i want the dog to see him do it.

closing in the dog doesnt look like it intends to move.
we flank big on either side.
i already tried pointing the trainer at him with no response.
now i cock it back, ready to strike.
he understands that and moves aside for us.
he rushes at us a couple of times as we pass
but i raise the trainer, and dale cocks his arm, and the dog backs
down each time.

130

we are relieved once we pass the husky.
9 miles down, how many dog encounters?
we'll be on the highway soon, and altho neither of us have done
the first mile of it recently,
dogs are not usually an issue near a highway.

we think it is all behind us.

it hasn't even started.

dale and i are walking along talking at about 10 miles
and we see some people at a construction site on the hillside
across short creek.
then we hear dogs barking and a bunch of dogs come tearing
down the hill.

1, 2, 3, 4, 5, 6

six big dogs.
not good.

the owner yells and whistles at them,
but the dogs pay no heed.
the dogs cross the creek.

i can see the owner coming after them,
but he won't reach the road until whatever happens is over.
up the hill toward the road they come.
i can see dale moving away from me and big.
"i've got it, big" i tell my dog,
but i am not sure.

usually in dealing with a pack, you are just dealing with one dog.
turn that dog, and you turn the pack.
of all things, the lead dog is an irish wolfhound.
it is a huge dog, bred to kill.
and i know next to nothing about the breed.
i am confident i can land the first blow with the trainer,
but i am not sure that will be enough.
the good thing about the trainer is that,
while it deals a painful blow,

it usually does no real damage.
i do not know if that will be enough to stop this dog.
at the moment i would prefer to have a gun.
the next 3 dogs are some kind of golden long haired dogs about
german shepherd size.
i don't know what breed they are.
the last two are bringing up the rear.
they are big, but everything is going to be decided by what
happens with the lead dogs.
i don't pay any attention to the trailers.
i just hope the whole pack will stop at the fence.

they don't.
there is this electric moment when you know that it is all on the
line. everything is suddenly incredibly crystal clear.
it is like the action slows down and you can see everything
and your mind is analyzing and making decisions instantly.
thought and action coalesce into a single unit.

someone is going to get hurt right now.

it might be me and big,
but not if i can help it.
it is on.

the irish wolfhound hits the road at full speed and bores down
straight at big and me.
two of the golden dogs split to the right to come around us, one
to the left.
i step into the wolfhound and bring the trainer around with full
force in one motion.
this is not what he expected and he starts to stop just as the end
of the trainer smacks into the side of his head with a loud crack.
his head snaps sideways, he lets out a yelp and turns,
but i am already on to the other dogs.

somehow i can see them all at once.
the dog on our left is turning away,
and one of the dogs on the right is turning away,
but the third golden dog is turning towards us and is almost on
big's unprotected flank.

132

god bless the big guy for his faith in me.
he isn't protecting himself, he is watching my feet and moving
out of my way so he doesn't trip me up.
the trainer lands full force into the face of the last threat,
within a foot of the big,
and i see teeth fly and hear another yelp.

it has probably been less than 3 seconds since the dogs hit the
road, and they are all running away.

i feel a little sick to my stomach as i watch the yellow dog flee.
he is holding his head funny, and one whole side of his face
seems to be hanging down.
i might have messed him up bad.

immediately my mind is running thru the whole scene again.
was he turning to flee and just unlucky to turn into us?
or was he taking aim on my big guy's backside?
did i have to hit him?

i just don't know.
there is no way to ever know.
in a battle you just have to defend yourself.

the owner reaches the creek coming towards us
at the same time as the fleeing dogs reach it heading for home,
and pauses to throw a couple of rocks at them,
to go with the curses.
then he climbs on up to the other side of the fence.

i take pre-emptive action,
altho i know he was not happy to see his dogs attack us.
"i'm sorry, i might have hurt the yellow dog."
not exactly true. i knew i had hurt the dog.
"no, i'm sorry, they shouldn't have come after you. we just didn't
expect to see someone come by on foot."

he was probably about as scared as i was, thinking he was gonna
see his dogs kill someone.
the funny thing was, i hadn't been scared they would hurt me.
i was scared they'd hurt big.

i choose to run the roads, and i know the risks.
big was there because he trusted me.

we talked a few minutes and i gave him my name and phone
number. he was doing drystonework, and there aren't many of us
around who can do it.
i told him i wasn't as young as i used to be and couldn't do as
much as i used to do.
but i'd discount my rate.
that's true. i can't do enough now to make a living at it.
but any income beats none.

after we moved on,
dale said he couldn't believe how disciplined big was.
"through that whole thing he never even growled. he was just
watching you."
"he's good about that. keeps him from tripping me up."

i was proud of my boy,
but having a hard time getting the image of that yellow dog out of
my head.

of course, the dog trials weren't quite over.
we passed a chained up pit bull neat the end of the run.
the boy who owns him was in the yard with some friends and i
heard one of his buddies say;
"...let him run around a little bit..."

fully alert, i looked, and sure enough he was heading over to
release his pit bull.
every time i walk by with big or little,
that dog rages and charges the end of his chain.

"why don't you let us get past before you let him loose?"
"huh?"
"why don't you let us get down the road before you let him
loose?"
"oh. yeah, ok."

and, of course, there was lynnor's nasty little pug.

so there it was.
about once every 10 years i have a truly serious dog encounter.
the nuisances are constant
but the serious encounters are rare.
never the less, i plan to continue to be prepared every time i go
out the door.

oh, yeah.
big set a pr. 12 miles is his longest day yet.
and when we got home he was running around in the yard
playing!

dale, on the other hand, asked where he could get a dog trainer.

laz

## march 03, 2012
## big relationships

relationships are important in big's world.
he has a need to know where everyone else fits in.
ben has become his buddy.
whenever we encounter ben,
be it running on the road or working on the fences on his farm
(cleaning out fencerows is a job that never ends)
big makes himself available for petting,
and ben always obliges.
big even got over shying away from the dog stick ben carries
running
(an ultimate measure of big trust)

now that dale has become a semi-regular training partner
(dale is training for his first half-marathon)
big has pretty much adopted him.
he thinks dale needs a coach.

the first time dale met big on the road, big was running with amy.
dale told me later;
"i kept a safe distance. big didn't do anything but look at me,
but i could see that he was telling me if i got too close to amy he
would bite my face off."
i laughed and told dale that was probably his "are you going to
pet me?" look, combined with his "are you going to hit me with
that stick?" look.

when we trained together the first time,
big was pretty leery of dale; until dale left his dog stick behind.
(see people, it isn't just me. no one runs out here without a dog
weapon)
after that, big took the lead as chief rattlesnake scout and set a
nice even pace for us.
it wasn't until dale turned to go to his house that big got
disturbed.

he tried to get me to go with dale,
he took a few steps after dale.

then he looked at me. then he looked at dale.
then he looked back at me and whined.

when that didn't work he kept his head turned,
watching for glimpses of dale across the hayfield and thru the
trees as our roads diverged further and further.
he kept looking up at me with distress,
wanting me to fix things and get dale back.
when we find a runner on the road, big wants to take them home.
"can i keep him?"

i had this picture in my mind of dale calling home & saying;
"linda, i'm gonna be late. i'll have to sneak out after big goes to
sleep."

now, when we see dale coming, big goes into john deere mode.
he can't wait to lean his enormous head on dale's leg to get
petted.
i "could" restrain him, but it isn't worth the effort.
i just hang on and take the ride.

the first time he did that dale laughed.
"if big had done that the day i met him, i would have died of a
heart attack!"

and the big team just keeps growing.
jeff, down the road, had a real heart attack recently.
his dr told him to walk 5 minutes a day for exercise.
jeff said;
"five minutes? i'm not putting on my shoes to walk five minutes!
i'll start with a mile."

me and big found him walking down the road the other day.
i hurried to catch up.
ok, big hurried me to catch up
(altho i didn't allow him to go into john deere mode)
he's gotten so used to finding "runners" on the road now
that he didn't even worry about jeff's dog stick.
he just made himself available to be petted.
and jeff obliged.

138

then big took up rattlesnake duty on the point and we walked.
of course everything was fine until jeff turned into his driveway.
big looked at jeff walking away,
then he looked up at me;
"i thought you'd let me keep this one?"

we had a real treat last sunday afternoon.
the dirt family came to visit.
dirt and eva and marshall.

as long as i have known dirt,
we hadn't gotten to get together much the last couple of years.
marshall is at the activity age and i think all parents know what
that means.

so dirt hadn't met the big yet.
i wasn't sure what big would think.
dirt is a lot bigger than the people he is used to.
dirt is one of those 6-6 guys that looks a lot taller.
(in basketball coach talk he is a "long" player)

the only similar size person he has seen was wayne,
when the nba players were here
(at 6-9 and 300+ a lot, wayne is an 'ex' nba player)
wayne was not at all comfortable with big and big was unnerved
by that.
(wayne was the only one that would even go in the yard with
him- they all thought amy was wonder woman to run with him)
for the remainder of their stay, wayne and all the nba guys
checked the yard to be sure big was attached to his cable
before they would leave the house to get in their cars.

big sniffed a hand and let dan pet him once,
but he wasn't totally comfortable.
he hid behind my legs and even growled a low growl.

so dan and i returned to the porch.
all the adults were talking while marshall was playing in the
yard, and running up and down a pile of dirt and rock that i am
mining for building materials.

after a little while eva asked;
"should marshall be doing that with big?"
"is he petting him?"
"yes"
"then he is fine"
having overcome his fear of children, big likes them almost as
well as he likes the ladies.
ok, he likes them just as much,
but he saves his flirting moves for the ladies.

then marshall came and asked if we could walk on the trails.
sure; it hadn't rained for a few days (for a change) and they were
probably dry enough to walk.
dan asked if big could go.
"big would love that"
dan walked around the corner and held up big's leash;
"look what i've got!"

big hesitated only a second, then his face lit up;
"well, why didn't you say so before!!"
dan gets an honorary degree in dog psychology...
and a prime spot on the big team.

we did have to pause partway down the drive
and make big "stop" and "sit"
so i could explain to him that he isn't allowed to pull dan any
more than he is allowed to pull me.
after that we had a great walk.

marshall understood how the trail was meant to be used.
he jumped up on the rocks, he jumped down off the rocks,
he ran and jumped from rock to rock.
"this is a great trail!"

there were rocks and more rocks.
eva appreciated how the trail was designed.
we crossed every rock ledge where there were natural steps next
to the jumps...
for those of us whose jumping days are past.

big did rattlesnake duty and dirt just followed.

140

big knows the trails like the back of his paw.
we did the little loop from down by the road to behind the house,
then we did the endless loop.
marshall got to take big for a while.
altho he probably outweighed marshall,
big was a perfect gentleman.
he seems to understand that he can't pull little people
(sorry amy)

by the time we finished the endless loop,
big and dirt had gotten a ways ahead.
we came to where we could see the trail all the way back to the
house, and there was no sign of big and dirt.

"DAN!"
"YES?"

the answer came from down a side trail.
they had started off on the endless loop again.

"YOU'RE GOING THE WRONG WAY!"
"I'M JUST FOLLOWING BIG!"
"IF YOU FOLLOW BIG, YOU'LL NEVER FINISH!"

coach big never chooses the turn that ends the workout.
he doesn't believe in shortened workouts any more than he
believes in tapering or days off.
but he does believe in relationships.

fortunately he didn't see the dirt family when they had to leave.
big loves his people, but in his world people sometimes leave and
never come back.

he has conquered a lot of fears,
but that one runs awful deep.

laz

## postscript
## Re: The Big Half Marathon

I have been following the Big stories since their beginning and have started several times lately to write to Laz and congratulate him on becoming a dog handler. Not too many people reach the level of training and understanding that Laz and Big have achieved - even professional handlers don't always get there.

I started working law enforcement bloodhounds in 1982 and was a handler until retirement in 1993. I've been a SAR dog handler since 1996 and just lost my partner of 16 years this January.

I back Laz 100% on his actions - to me he read the situation correctly and responded in an appropriate manner. Had I been in his shoes I would have done the exact same thing - and worse if possible.

As to Big's behavior during the incident - it shows only the level of training and trust achieved. Not a one of the dogs that I have worked in the last 30 years would have reacted any different than Big. Laz is the pack leader, the alpha, and Big waits to see what the leader wants done. My old girl would wait beside me if we were challenged by other dogs, should I holler and become upset she would offer to eat them alive for me. If I stayed calm she would only watch closely until we were safely past the threat. Big trusts Laz to call the shots...

So, congratulations Laz ! You've joined the ranks of dog handlers. It's an honorary title bestowed by your dog's behavior. His obedience to you, his trust in you and the remarkable communication that you two share show that it is a title well deserved - Big is your partner.

Jo D.

(And, yes, I have met both Laz and Big)

# About the Author

Lazarus Lake did not write this book; he merely recorded the stories that Big shared with him. They live on a farm in Tennessee where they train and organize popular ultra-marathons, a world-wide community that Laz has been a part of for over 3 decades and Big first joined a couple of years ago.

# About the Illustrator

Betsy Julian lives with her musician husband, striped cat, and opinionated cockatiel in the hills of East Tennessee. She has a BFA and a MS in Education. Her art is inspired by traditional Appalachian applied arts. Most of the time she can be found in a ceramics studio or teaching high school art.

Made in the USA
San Bernardino, CA
26 November 2016